Companions in Hope

The Art of Christian Caring

Robert J. Wicks and Thomas E. Rodgerson

PAULIST PRESS
New York/Mahwah, N.J.

Cover design by Moe Berman

Library of Congress Cataloging-in-Publication Data

Wicks, Robert J.
    Companions in hope : the art of Christian caring / Robert J. Wicks and Thomas E. Rodgerson.
        p. cm.
    Includes bibliographical references.
    ISBN 0-8091-3781-X (alk. paper)
    1. Caring—Religious aspects—Christianity. I. Rodgerson, Thomas E., 1950–   . II. Title.
BV4647.S9W53   1998
241'.4—dc21   97-50313
                                                                                          CIP

Published by Paulist Press
997 Macarthur Boulevard
Mahwah, New Jersey 07430

Printed and bound in the
United States of America

Contents

DEDICATION

For
Marie Gipprich,
a beautiful person of hope
—R.J.W.

To
Bev,
my companion in hope
—T.E.R.

1. Introduction

Opportunities abound for caring in the fabric of everyday life where simple words are spoken by friends, where a troubled facial expression is noticed by a sensitive acquaintance, or an aware spouse picks up on an unusual intensity of emotion. In these simple, everyday moments there can occur a form of caring that helps to alleviate the suffering of another person and has the potential for the transformation of that person as he or she gains new insights about life or chooses to think and act in new ways. Such caring has the potential to set people free and to enable them to live more complete lives as children of God.

Yet many of these opportunities are missed. Perhaps our eyes and ears are not trained to see the importance of these simple opportunities, or maybe there is a natural sensitivity to these opportunities that has been dulled over time by the rush of responsibility and the need to survive. Perhaps we have noticed special occasions when someone close (a child, parent, spouse, employee, friend) has reached out to us because of an inability to cope, but we felt awkward and ill-equipped to do anymore than give some trite advice.

Most of us have healthy personalities and effective interpersonal styles that give us a natural basis for a type of caring that is transformational. We simply need additional guidance to extend our natural abilities in helping others. Today there is a plethora of aids for almost every problem—how-to manuals that range from macramé and vegetable growing to building your own vacation home and saving your marriage. Today, too, the ranks of professional counselors and therapists have swelled tremendously, as has the number of books on self-help and enlightenment, pop psychology, and meditation. Yet there is little written on how we can care for our family, friends, neighbors and business colleagues when they are anxious, depressed or hurting. Even less is written on how such caring can be an important part of the spiritual growth of these persons.

One businessman said many of his coworkers come to him for support. Although he believed he could help them, he expressed dismay at the lack of down-to-earth books available to help him to be more effective and intentional in his caring.

A mother once exclaimed, "I have a depressed neighbor. She comes to me and I don't know what to say to her. Is there anything I can do besides merely hearing her out and eventually saying, 'Go seek help elsewhere'?"

And what about our families—both our biological families and our families in the faith? Constantly we must deal with an angry child, a distant adolescent or a temporarily upset spouse. And in the community of faith there are constant misunderstandings and disagreements. Isn't there something we can learn about caring that will enable us to truly help others and not miss these opportunities for spiritual growth?

In a society in which alienation and isolation are becoming more and more prevalent, helping other people reach out more effectively to their family, friends and business acquaintances is not merely a desirable undertaking—it is an essential, humane pursuit. As families become smaller, cities and businesses become larger, schools begin numbering us and the demand for job mobility increases, our support systems shrink. When we get depressed, we find there is no one to hear us cry; when we get angry, there are few people to turn to who will let us scream out; when we get confused amidst difficult life choices, there is rarely someone able to help us get our bearings straight. And when we feel the stress of modern existence and the pain of troubled personal relations, we often look in vain for that special someone who will care.

Companions in Hope is written as a partial antidote to the isolation and potential alienation of people in a world that is moving too fast and, in the process, rapidly discouraging people from fulfilling their human and spiritual responsibilities to each other. It is written with the belief that ordinary people need to be considered as a critical component to the healing team of caring professionals that includes clergy, therapists and doctors. This is not to say that such people in their everyday lives would take the place of these professionals, but that they would be acknowledged in their important roles as gatekeepers who are often the first to see evidence of distress in others and are the first to decide if such distress deserves a call to a helping professional. Further, they need to be acknowledged in their critical roles of providing preventive and strategic care.

The idea of preventive care is certainly in keeping with past developments in preventive psychiatry and community psychology. The establishment of local community health clinics and the hiring of competent, caring paraprofessionals with bachelors' degrees or less is based on the well-founded belief that professionals cannot and need not do it alone.

There is nothing wrong with reaching out for help to a professional. In many instances they are needed as supportive, objective helpers. In our age of specialization, though, there seems to be an increasing trend to use hotlines, psychotherapists, counselors and psychopharmacologic drugs instead of first turning to family and friends. Yet, often, particularly in a minor crisis, colleagues, family or friends could have provided the needed help.

More recent trends of budget cutting of social programs and the limiting of benefits for mental health by insurance companies increase the importance of the role of family and friends in preventive and strategic care. Others have long called for the community of faith to play a leading role in the mental health of our communities.[1] Increasingly, this may not be just a call, but a necessity. Will we be equipped to do it? And is this not the recovery of a task that has historically been chosen by the community of faith (and not just the clergy)—namely, to provide preventive care (warding off more serious physical, emotional, spiritual crises) and strategic care (directly helping the poor, sick and needy, and also setting standards for right living through teaching and by example)?[2]

Insights gained in the development of pastoral counseling as a profession now need to be shared with the wider faith community to enhance the historic role of every believer as a giver of preventive and strategic care and, in a similar fashion, to enhance the historic role of the faith community as a key provider of mental health resources for the wider community. Insights gained from the profession of pastoral counseling can help us avoid missing the opportunities for caring that will often lead to moments of transformation.

Pastoral counseling as a profession has emerged from an integration of sound theology and well-grounded psychology. As in all counseling, the goal is understanding, but in pastoral counseling the understanding achieved is sought as a basis for conversion. The focus in pastoral counseling is to help people better understand their relationships with themselves and the world, with an eye to the influence that God is having in their lives. In addition to seeking to understand appropriate clinical theory and skills, the pastoral counselor takes into account such elements as: (1) seeking spiritual equanimity or standing with persons as they face the mystery of pain; (2) seeing growth as taking place in a community of faith as well as helping the community to grow; (3) uncovering the healing presence of God; (4) having a sincere appreciation of grace that engenders hope and helps us to accept our limits; and (5) seeking justice that is grounded in God's will for humanity.[3]

Based upon the insights gained from the profession of pastoral counseling and upon the belief that everyone in the community of faith can participate in a form of caring that is transformational, *Companions in Hope* provides practical information on how to better interact with others on a daily basis as empathetic, caring people. This book does not make light of emotional distress or provide a superficial view of personal difficulties. Nor is this book designed to turn the reader into a professional counselor. Instead, it is designed to enhance personal talents in the areas of listening, being supportive, problem-solving, dealing with crises and knowing when and how to refer, in order to equip an army of caregivers who might work to facilitate spiritual growth on a broad level.

2. Caring to Listen: Overcoming Resistance

We cannot care without listening. If we do not listen, we do not care. Dietrich Bonhoeffer stated that the first service we owe to others in fellowship is to listen to them. If we fail to listen, there are spiritual consequences because as he says, "...he who can no longer listen to his brother will soon be no longer listening to God either."[1]

Yet, true listening does not necessarily come naturally and must be distinguished from simply hearing. During the course of a day we hear many sounds, but only *listen* to a few. Hearing is an easy, passive process. Listening requires energy, motivation and patience.

Trying to make sense of the numerous facts and issues contained in every communication is extremely difficult. That is why, when another person bombards us with a multitude of thoughts, problems and emotions, we often respond by becoming lazy or disinterested. As this happens, we lower our attention thresholds, turn our minds to other thoughts and put on our "Oh yes, of course I'm interested" facial masks.

Sometimes we do not listen because we are too preoccupied with our own issues to listen. Sometimes we do not listen because we lack the skills to listen. Often we do not listen because there are inner pressures that arise within us and block our abilities to truly listen. What comes across as laziness or disinterest may have more to do with our own anxieties about listening, with our own struggles to have the right answers and with the emotions and silences that emerge when we cannot give a quick fix.

Embarrassingly, we may get caught in our halfhearted listening. But more importantly, we have missed these opportunities to participate in significant moments in the lives of other people. This is a shame, and it is one of the reasons why so many people turn to professionals for help. It is also why many turn to alcohol, drugs, fantasy or decide to turn off life completely. If no one bothers to listen to us (no matter how many people are physically present in our environment), the usual ensuing feeling is *loneliness.* And the simple fact is that being alone can be scary.

Children in trouble often tell of being alienated from their own families at the very time when they most need the care that is conveyed through listening:

"I tried to talk to my parents about sex but they wouldn't hear of it. Each time I brought up the issue of birth control, they would respond by saying, 'Are you sleeping around, Robin? If we find out that you are, you're going to be in a good deal of trouble! I don't know where you get all of these questions, but I'm sure it's those sluts you hang around with after school.' So I just stopped bringing it up."

"So, you found out about sex from...?"

"Well, I got tired of being harassed by my parents, so I asked my 'slutty friends.' And they told me to take the pill if I was going to do something."

"And?"

"Well, how was I to know you were supposed to take it every day? I felt stupid enough asking them....They laughed at me as it was. And when Mary got some, there were no instructions. So I just took them anytime Billy and I would sleep together. So when I found out I was pregnant I couldn't figure out what I had done wrong...."

"How did your parents react?"

"They went wild, called me everything in the book, and—you're not going to believe this—when they calmed down, my mother asked me, 'How come you didn't come to us sooner?'"

Why had Robin's parents closed the lines of caring communication? Surely not out of malice, but probably out of anxiety.

Overcoming Anxiety

Anxiety is one of the leading blocks to effective listening. It can affect both the person listening and the person seeking assistance.

The distressed person can experience a high degree of anxiety just by telling his/her story, no matter how motivated this person may be to share the burden. Even when the two people involved know each other, such anxiety may be present.

"But I thought you said your neighbor was usually pretty sympathetic; yet you held back quite a bit when you told her about your husband's health...."

"I started to tell her. I started to tell her each time I went over there, but...well, I just couldn't get it out. I was afraid she wouldn't understand, that she would think I didn't care about my husband and his feelings if I spent time going into how I felt and how his problems upset me."

In listening to someone relate a problem, therefore, we must realize and accept that they may be anxious. It's a natural reaction since we are all concerned with how we come across and are received.

A similar nervousness may also exist in the person who wants to have a listening and caring presence. One popular quote still heard in psychotherapy seminars is, "It's all right if one of the persons in the therapist's office is anxious—as long as it isn't the therapist." Accordingly, much time is spent by trainees in analyzing those things that might make the novice psychiatrist, psychologist, clinical social worker or pastoral counselor nervous when dealing with a patient.

When we care to listen to someone with a problem, we may actually feel their anxiety when in their presence. This gives us a clue to their feelings, and we can work to put them at ease. But often the anxiety we feel rises from *our own* internal pressures. First, we may be concerned, like most caring listeners, about whether or not we will say or do something wrong. The feeling is, "If I don't say something, she'll think I don't understand; and if I do say something, she'll know it for sure!" Often this is tied to an internal pressure that we must fix the problem that is presented to us, or somehow make it better. There is an assumption here that we are supposed to know how to deal with any problem and come up with exactly the right words. Yet, if we unwittingly make that assumption, we actually eclipse the role of the Savior in the caring process and suffer ourselves from the "savior complex."

Second, if we take ourselves out of the savior role, then other internal pressures emerge from within us that cause anxiety. What if they stop talking and we have nothing to say? How will we endure the silence? What if they become emotional as they talk and we begin to feel emotions of our own? What if they touch on topics with which we are uncomfortable, like death, anger, love or sex? What if, in the end, there are no clear answers that emerge when we care to listen, and we are left with uncertainty? Have we really been of any help then?

Of course, another one of our assumptions is that all this anxiety is bad. Initially, when we care to listen, it is awkward to experience both the anxiety of another person as well as our own anxiety. Yet another way to think of anxiety is that it is wonderful. It is a wonderful clue. Our perception of anxiety is a clue that something important is happening here. Where anxiety is, there is always opportunity. Our inner self is telling us that we are on "holy ground." We are entering into one of those meaningful moments where creation actually happens; where, for a moment, the otherwise rigid inner structures of the self become more pliable, and both the one listening and the one speaking have the opportunity to grow. Is it not true that, whenever God is about to do something new in creation, the human response is that of anxiety, and that the angels are sent first to say, "Be not afraid!"?

Anxiety gets our attention. Our attitude becomes, "This is a special moment." Our approach becomes that of one who is very interested to see what will emerge. And then we can go forward with confidence, remembering the words of our Lord to the disciples who were anxious about their own transforming presence before the authorities of the day: "…do not be anxious how or what you are to answer or what you are to say; for the Holy Spirit will teach you in that very hour what you ought to say" (Luke 12:11–12).

Overcoming the Savior Complex

Homo sapiens is distinguished from other species in the animal kingdom by a number of characteristics. While a positive one is our sense of humor, a negative one surely is our tendency to feign omnipotence in dealing with others.

Humility is a rare, special trait among human beings; pomposity and arrogance, unfortunately, are less rare. That is why constructive feedback from family, friends and peers is necessary if our estimation of ourselves is to retain some sort of basis in reality. Many "self-help" or "pop psychology" authors might disagree with this point of view. They would say, "You should be more assertive! Say 'no' to others! Get what's coming to you! You're not pompous, they are!" However, this is far from true. Even in the case of shy persons, it is their self-centeredness that sometimes gets them into trouble.

Shy people are used as an example here because they seem, by virtue of their very diffident behavior, to be the complete antithesis of pomposity. By looking more deeply, though, we can see that this is not completely true. If shy people weren't so convinced that *everyone* was looking at them when they walked into a room and that *everyone* would notice if they made a mistake in a conversation or social interaction, they would be more active and loquacious. In this sense they have an inflated view of themselves and of the size of the impact they make on others.

Now if shy people have problems with inflated self-images, how about us outgoing souls? Moreover, if anything inflates the ego, it is having one of our peers come to us with a problem or to vent feelings of frustration. The first thought striking many of us is, "My goodness, he's coming to *me* for help. He must think I'm quite knowledgeable. Isn't that great?" Yet that thought barely gets a chance to brighten up our self-image before fear overtakes us with the dispiriting question, "What can I do for this person?"—the implicit thought being, "Boy, is he going to be disappointed," or "Am I going to look bad!"

Then, with this negative feeling thoroughly imbedded, we quite naturally do one of two inappropriate things. Either we try to beg off by assuming the attitude of, "After all, what can I possibly do to help?" Or else we put on our "savior" mantle and try to heal the other person by offering advice and wise words that are designed to "lift the spirit" or be the perfect solution to his or her problem.

In both instances, the person who is seeking help loses because he or she is either rejected or smothered with "golden" and often useless words of wisdom. We, the designated helpers, also lose when we leave the situation feeling frustrated because our help "didn't do the trick," or feeling guilty because we neglected to offer help at all.

This is a truly unfortunate situation because, with a little awareness of ourselves and others, this frustrating outcome is normally unnecessary and avoidable. In reality, when someone comes to us for aid, they are usually only asking us to be supportive and a good listener. Having someone who will listen without judging, ignoring or providing nicely packaged cures is in itself a great joy.

We can work to overcome the "savior complex" by first recognizing this tendency in ourselves. We can monitor those thoughts that reflect pride or a pressure to perform. We can monitor our replies that either brush people off or offer quick solutions. We can notice that this approach simply does not help (usually by experiencing this unhelpful approach ourselves when all that we really want is someone to listen). We can choose to become interested in the silence, the emotion and the ambiguity that emerge when we cease to play savior.

Enduring Silence

People in general have great difficulty dealing with silence, especially their own. This means that a good listener is a rarity. Being silent is not easy. As a matter of fact, it is actually discouraged in modern society. Our cars are not complete without radios, tape decks or CD players. Our homes are filled with the sounds of television, stereos and rented movies, and at a party we are considered quite the person if we can pick up the ball when there is a lull in the verbal action. Even in contemporary religious services, sounds abound: we are either preached or sung to, or are busy doing the same ourselves as part of the congregation. Quiet meditation is something of an oddity. Therefore, for many people remaining silent is not easy. Today's societal conditioning militates against it. The value of being silent is almost obscured in our action-oriented times.

The feeling is that, unless we are *doing* something, we are useless. Unfortunately this fits in with the "savior complex," which dictates that we should rescue those seeking to share their problems with us. The negative result is that we fail to be silent with someone who comes to us feeling a bit down, distressed or frustrated. This is sad because they want us to listen. They want to unburden themselves. They want to open up and share their thoughts. This process is impossible if they are only met with talk, talk and more talk.

A neighbor may say, "I really feel down. I don't know what to do"—and they remain silent. A friend may say the following before lapsing into silence, "My daughter is really getting the best of me." Or a family member may say, "Grandpa is not fair to me. I'm tired of listening to it"—with a long pause after the statement.

In such instances, it may not seem that the person is going to follow with an elaboration, but that is just what is needed if the listener is to be of some help. Accordingly, when people start with statements like the ones made above, the caring listener has two natural choices: either to remain silent or to indicate briefly to the other person to continue ("You've been feeling down lately...? What's been happening with your daughter? What's Grandpa been doing?").

Once this encouragement has been given to the person, remaining silent and waiting for the person to elaborate is usually a safe and appropriate technique. When people are ready to open up, they will. Occasionally, further prompting is necessary, but this is rare. It is usually a mistake not to practice patience and perseverance. Often it is the *listener's* difficulty with silence that prompts giving further encouragement to speak rather than the actual need to give such encouragement.

After the person has begun, we may also encounter periods of silence. This can occur for any number of reasons. It may be that the individual is thinking about what to say next; she's angry, confused, embarrassed or is waiting to see our reaction. At such a time, unless it is a natural break and it really is time to say something, waiting is best. Waiting is not easy, even for the experienced listener. As was indicated, due to the habit of responding in conversation and our general discomfort with silence, it is quite natural to feel under great pressure to speak up when someone else stops.

Holding back can have great benefits, though. By not responding, a vacuum is set up within which the person can think, have the opportunity to continue, change the topic, vent emotions or just enjoy the comfort of another person's presence. By controlling ourselves, we give them the freedom to express themselves.

Theodor Reik calls this the "power of silence."[2] He says that people actually come to us as caring listeners with material that for them has remained silent. They have often told no one. Ironically, it is our ability to remain silent that drives people deep into their own unspoken or unspeakable layers of being and forces them to put words to their silent material. This principle is often seen in the scriptures, especially in the psalms of lament, where God chooses to be silent in the face of the psalmist's pain. In the silence, the psalmist finds words for the heretofore unspeakable suffering. Speaking the unspeakable out of the silence seems to be profoundly therapeutic.

Even in a casual setting we can experiment with this principle. In a normal conversational setting, instead of being talkative, try using a "quiet approach." When someone is talking, instead of breaking in if you have a question, as you normally do, wait and remain silent. See what happens.

When we hold ourselves back from interrupting someone with a question, or when we let a silent space go by without being the one to take control of it, it is amazing to see what happens. The other person often says something that sheds new light on his or her feelings or concerns about an issue.

One of the other reasons people have difficulty keeping silent during another person's narrative is that they feel they are not accomplishing anything. After all, what can caring individuals accomplish if they merely listen? This might be true if we were only passively listening to another's message. However, in the caring process we employ "active listening."

Active listening is not just patiently keeping our mouth shut until the opportunity arises to break in and share our words of wisdom. Rather, it is a process in which we are trying to put together the whole message the person is sending. It is a method of taking what the person is saying to us now and trying to fit it into the pattern of what they have been trying to convey the whole time they have been with us.

If we just listen in a passive way and spend this time trying to figure out something terribly bright to say when we get the chance, much will be missed. Thus, ironically, when we do get any opportunity to provide our pearls of wisdom, we probably will say something that misses the mark by a mile.

Paul Williams, the composer and singer, wrote on the back of one of his early albums: "There are those who listen, and those who wait to talk. This album is dedicated to the listeners." One could paraphrase this in reference to all caring listeners, whether professional or not. "There are those who actively listen, and those who merely hear. Caring is done by real listeners."

Enduring Emotions

When we care to listen, not looking for a quick fix and not filling the silences, emotions will often emerge that silence tends to exaggerate. It was Shakespeare who wrote, "Short time seems long in sorrow's sharp sustaining." When someone begins to cry or to express intense anger, seconds can seem like hours when there really isn't anything to say.

In these moments there is an internal pressure that arises, tempting us to step out of the listening role. Our fear is often that the emotions will get out of control. Will the emotions get even more intense? Will the person "lose it" or will we "lose it"? These are moments when we are tempted to change the subject or quickly pacify the emotion so the person will get over it.

While it seems almost instinctual to quell the rising tide of any emotion, actually doing the opposite is most helpful. We may, in fact, be helping a person not to "lose it" by letting him or her go

ahead and talk out the emotion now. We can offer simple statements that encourage the person to go further. In the midst of a
flow of tears we can simply say, "I hear your pain," or "Can you
put any words to your tears?" Or we can simply remain silent. In
a flurry of anger we can simply say, "I hear the intensity of your
anger," or even, "It sounds like some of that anger is for me."

The person in pain will let us know when he/she is finished
with the emotion. The storm of emotion will pass. And by remaining as a caring listener, the message will be conveyed to this person that his/her emotions are valid and that he/she can trust the
process of expressing those emotions in a safe environment.

Intense emotional moments can arise at any time. In the
simple act of going to visit a person who has been absent from
the church for a while, we can often catch a surprising amount of
emotion (Is this why very few in the church will ever get the
courage to go visiting?). We knock on the door and encounter a
woman who has suffered the loss of a family member and, since
she was not a regular attendee, no one in the church knew about
it and no one came to express sympathy. But now we arrive as
representatives of the church and as representatives of Christ.
Before we can get to the intense pain of the loss, there is a flurry
of anger that is directed right at us. We can defend and apolo-
gize. We can quickly leave. We can blame it on one of the pastors.
Or we can be caring listeners, hearing the anger, inviting her to
go further and standing with her in the disappointment. After
the anger she can talk about the pain of losing the family member. Maybe after that, she can begin to talk about putting her life
back together or seeing what the future holds.

In the intensity of emotions, often exacerbated by silence,
our own emotions rise to the surface too. We may not be at all
comfortable with our own emotions. Will our own emotions get
out of control? Will the other person notice?

Ironically, we are more likely to "lose it" (now or in the
future) if we deny our emotions. A more useful approach is to
intentionally observe and use our own emotions when we
assume the roles of the listeners who care.

We can use our emotions as a clue to what the other person
is experiencing. We can empathetically respond simply because

our own emotions have given us a hint at what the other person is feeling—and we do not necessarily have to say anything to convey this. We are often tempted to share a story of our own that conveys our similar emotion. Sometimes this is appropriate if is kept brief and only after the other person has talked through his or her emotion. However, generally it is best to keep the focus on the other person lest the listening role reverses and he or she ends up bearing the pain of our story.

We can use our own emotions as a means for personal growth. When our own emotions seem intense or a particular topic makes us feel uncomfortable, we can take note of our reactions. Later we can ask ourselves, "I wonder why this touched me the way it did? What am I not finished with that is touched by this?" We may want to process our feelings later with our own caring listener.

Finally, we can use our own emotions to acknowledge our own humanness. In the face of Lazarus's death and the pain of Mary and Martha, Jesus wept (John 11:35). Sometimes we need to let our emotions show and trust that God can use that, too, in the healing process.

Enduring Ambiguity

Sometimes there are no answers. Sometimes the choices are impossible, or there is really no choice at all. In the movie "Sophie's Choice," a mother forced onto a death train in Nazi Germany arrives at a concentration camp with her two children. As she gets off the train a soldier says that she has to choose only one child to go with her. In the agony of the moment that scars her for life, she chooses to take her daughter, hoping that her son will be able to take care of himself. Sophie's choice is really no choice at all. Nothing seems clear. How could we possibly advise Sophie on this choice? What could we say if we were the caring listener to whom she chose to tell her story?

The caring listener must be willing to endure the ambiguity of the moment where there are no answers. We must be willing to step out of our black and white answers. We must be willing to question how we have given order to the universe, an order that begins to unravel in the face of a person's pain.

A couple who had waited and prayed to God for years finally gets pregnant. There are complications at childbirth. Two days later the child dies. There are no answers. Even the best listener will walk away knowing that the feelings are unresolved and wondering if there is any justice in the universe.

A woman sexually abused as a child wonders where God was and how a God of compassion could even allow such things to go on in creation. There are no answers. Feelings of hatred, betrayal or resentment are often left open like an oozing wound. How to think about God and how to order one's universe are often ambiguous. Statements like, "It was God's will," or "God will bring good out of this," are, at best, poor attempts to keep *our* universe orderly and, at worst, cruel responses. We have to be willing to endure the ambiguity.

Even in these moments, the caring listener has an important role that we must remember. In his book, *Till We Have Faces*, C. S. Lewis eloquently retells the myth of Cupid and Psyche.[3] The character Orual is the elder and ugly sister of the beautiful Psyche. Orual, in coming to grips with her ugliness, chooses to go through life with her face veiled. At the end of the story she stands before the gods, wanting to read her complaints about the injustices of life, about the ugliness of life when love is taken away by the gods. The gods strip off her veil and she stands with her ugly face uncovered, reading her ugly complaints about life. In the ugly complaining she finds her own real voice. The gods say nothing for a while and then ask her, "Are you answered?" And she says, "Yes."

What was the answer? As Orual says, "The complaint was the answer." The role of the caring listener in the face of life's ugliness is simply to hear the complaint. The complaint *is* the answer when there are no answers. The listener must learn to be content with nothing else and to see the value of hearing the complaint while having no answers.

Finally, when there are no answers the caring listener must remember that life is not about certainty. Life is about meaning. Pascal wrote in his *Penseés*, "We sail within a vast sphere, ever drifting in uncertainty, driven from end to end. When we think to attach ourselves to any point…it wavers and leaves us…."[4] Commenting on this passage from Pascal, Daniel Taylor in his book *The Myth of Certainty* says, "While certainty is beyond our reach, *meaning*—something far more valuable—is not. Meaning derives from a right relationship with God, based not on certainty and conformity, but on risk and commitment."[5]

When there are no answers, when the end is uncertain, we can still participate in a meaningful moment. Our listening, caring presence is often the catalyst for that meaningful moment. We are just there. This is meaningful to the person in pain. It happens because the listener has exhibited risk and commitment.

3. Caring to Listen: Standing on Holy Ground

When we commit to active listening, we soon learn that understanding others is, at best, a very complex undertaking. To understand other people as completely as possible, we must take special steps to meet them on their own ground. Their own "ground" is really "holy ground." We are like Moses, whose attention was caught by a burning bush, and as he drew near to the bush, he heard the word of God telling him to take off his shoes because the place on which he was standing was holy ground. When he acknowledged the sacredness of the place, he then received a profound revelation from God (Exodus 3:1–6).

Often our attention is caught by a burning issue in the life of a person, and we are urged to draw near. If we are not only to draw near but also to stay and truly hear the revealing words the person has to offer, then we, too, must meet her on her own "ground" and treat it as if it were "holy ground." We can do this by conveying an atmosphere of trust, by understanding her frame of reference, by recognizing her nonverbal signals, by evaluating our own reactions to what is being said and by keeping the focus on her even when her defensive style might push us away.

Conveying Trust

If we believe that we are drawing near to "holy ground" when we actively listen to a person, then we will automatically want to convey an atmosphere of trust. Where there is no trust, nothing sacred will be revealed. If the trust is at first given and is later betrayed, certainly nothing else sacred will ever be revealed.

18

Confidentiality is one of the keys to trust. Confidentiality is an explicit promise or contract to reveal nothing about a person except under conditions mutually agreed upon. For a counseling professional, this is a legal matter. By law, nothing can be shared outside of the counseling room unless a person is a danger to himself, or is intent on harming someone else or reveals information about child abuse. These limits to confidentiality are shared with the person before he tells his story. To a caring listener who is not in a professional role, this is an ethical matter. Without confidentiality, a person is not free to share deeply and personally. Without confidentiality, we cannot convey that his "ground" is "holy ground." While not legally required to report when a person is about to harm himself or another, or when information about child abuse is revealed, a nonprofessional caring listener would be well-advised to consult a professional in these matters and to convey such intentions to the person who is asking for care.

Trust is also conveyed by the caring listener who trusts in the process of active listening. Sometimes we think that we are conveying trust if we say, "Don't worry. Everything will be all right." Actually the opposite may be the case. We may be conveying that *we* do *not* trust enough to listen more deeply or to stay in the emotion. It is the nonanxious presence of one who is not afraid of silence or emotions or ambiguity (as pointed out in the previous chapter) that actually conveys the deepest sense of trust.[1] This nonanxious, caring listener is content with the active listening process and believes in its effectiveness, even though it is never predictable as to what will happen when we stand on "holy ground."

Finally, trust is conveyed by following some simple rules for active listening: (1) look at the person with whom you are talking; (2) allow for no distractions; (3) stop and think before responding; (4) wait for the other person to finish his/her thought before you start to talk or think about responding; (5) try to understand not just what is being said, but what the feeling is behind it; (6) look for important themes; (7) ask for clarification when needed; (8) temporarily suspend all judgment; (9) be patient as the person takes time to sort out thoughts and feelings.[2]

Adopting the Other's Frame of Reference

When a person comes for care, we treat his "ground" sacredly by trying to understand what he is saying from his point of view. While we may be attracted to him by his burning issue, we will not be able to (or allowed to) stay and truly hear what he has to say if we cannot grasp his frame of reference.

Whether we actually succeed in getting a good grasp of another's situation depends on a number of factors, but attempting to put ourselves in the other person's position is a major first step in gaining a better understanding of those who come to us in distress. If someone appears anxious about revealing a sensitive issue of a personal nature, we may take some steps to show we are in tune with the person and his current situation. We know that if we were in that position, we would want to take our time and not be rushed. With this in mind, special efforts can be made simply to allow the person to move ahead at a slow pace.

This may be the only thing that comes to mind. Still, even if it were the only way we could think of to reach out, it probably will make some type of positive impact.

No one can be *totally* empathetic. Thinking so is foolish and attempting to be so will be futile. Moreover, most people, with the exception of the very demanding, do not expect total empathy. They see as encouraging any sign that the person to whom they have come is simply making the effort to reach out in their direction.

This seems to hold true in any type of interpersonal encounter. If you are telling a joke, you appreciate the friend who is smiling in anticipation of the conclusion, as compared to old stoneface, who you know is not going to laugh no matter what.

In working toward getting a grasp of how the person feels in his/her current position, there are a number of simple steps we can take. Many of them we already take automatically. This is fine. The only drawback is that when we are not actively aware of these steps or techniques, we cannot guarantee their presence each time. Similarly, their implementation and improvement are sometimes stunted since they are given little attention.

In trying to grasp another person's position, ask yourself a number of questions:

How would you feel about sharing the kind of problem the other person is describing? How do you think that person feels about sharing it?

What would you expect of someone to whom you were relating a personal difficulty? What do you think the other person expects of you?

How could someone put you at ease? How might you put this person at ease?

It is important to cue in on the nonverbal signs and the kinds of things being said. By adding these impressions to your answers to the above questions, you will be better able to appreciate the other person's situation. Unless this effort is made, you run the risk of seeing the other person in a vacuum and losing sight of the human context of the situation.

If, for example, a youngster is telling you why he failed an exam, he might do a number of things. One of the things he might do is omit certain details that make him look bad. He might even distort certain factors to make his failure look reasonable.

Seeing his statement in a vacuum rather than in a human context (*his* context, or *his* "ground") might cause us to react to the omissions and distortions by saying, "Kenneth, you say you didn't have enough time to study, the teacher wasn't fair and there was material on the test that you hadn't been assigned. Whom do you think you're kidding? You'd better get your act together, mister—and fast!"

How do you think this youth will react? Probably the same way you and I did—with resentment. We felt we were not understood and saw our parents as tyrants. As we grew older, we saw that they had our best interests in mind, but some of us came to believe that setting limits did not have to take such a heartless form.

Furthermore, omitting things and providing minor distortions in portraying ourselves is something we all do. Suppose you were in a group setting and were asked to introduce yourself and say something about your background. Do you think you would tell potentially harmful things about yourself? "I'm a college graduate, mother of four, my husband is ugly and I stole apples from the fruit stand when I was eight years old." No way!

You, like practically everyone else, would be trying to impress your new acquaintances with how great you are. It's natural. It's human. So to condemn it in others is ridiculous.

Putting yourself in the other person's position can lead you to deal positively with what he or she is telling you. In the case of the youth who did poorly on his test, think of how he must be feeling. How did *you* feel when you did not do well in school? Then your handling of him might be more like the following:

"There seem to be a lot of reasons why you didn't do as well as you'd like. What can you do about it so you'll do better next time?"

"Well, I'd like to give that teacher a piece of my mind."

"I'm sure you would, but that wouldn't help. How could you alter your study habits so you're not caught off guard by a surprise test, or one that is more far-ranging than the lectures?"

In this interaction, the student is not being put on the defensive. Instead, he is being put at ease for a failure that cannot be changed, and prepped for having to take full responsibility for his next performance. Being able to identify with him and his situation, and with others who come to us with a difficulty, should help us in opening up new, constructive ways of handling such problems. When we join him on his "ground" as if it were "holy ground," new information emerges that may uncover new approaches or reveal deeper issues that may be blocking him from his full potential.

Recognizing Nonverbal Signs

To approach and stay with someone on her own "ground," which is "holy ground," we must not only use our ears, but also our other senses. We must not only use our ears, but also our eyes and our inner sense of what is happening in the room with a person if we are truly to understand her "ground." Using all of our senses, we learn to distinguish between the *manifest content* of what the person is conveying and the *total content* of the message being sent.

By manifest content, we mean the information contained in what a person says—that is, the meaning conveyed by the words alone. By total content, we are referring to the combined verbal and nonverbal message communicated by the person. This difference is quite important. Too often the messages that people verbalize are accepted at face value. They say they are sad and we sympathize; they indicate they are happy and we rejoice. We take what people say as being simple, straightforward and understandable. In doing this we are almost denying the complexity of the human being. The nuances of speech and the subtleties of human nature are being ignored.

It is true that when some people tell us they are happy, they are indeed quite happy. And the same goes for sadness or any other valued emotion. The problem arises when we accept the major parts of their messages but do not expend the energy to see if any contradictory points are being expressed. The richness of human feelings is expressed in the nuances and minor paradoxes that arise when we probe further into what people are trying to communicate. For example, someone who has admitted a past problem with drinking too much may quickly add that he or she seems to have it under control now, but may say so in a halting voice. If we ignore the dissonant tone reflected in the manner of speech, much will be lost from the communication.

Probably the primary reason we miss parts of someone's communication that may modify its meaning is our lack of motivation to pursue messages that puzzle us, or our lack of understanding of the nonverbal elements of communication. Paradoxically, this lack of understanding may be due in part to the heightened attention nonverbal communication has been given—and the subsequent discrediting of "body language."

In some instances the whole business of nonverbal communication has been overplayed. Some books tell us how much is revealed by the way one's leg crosses over the other, or how to tell another person's strong feelings for us by the way the individual is carrying himself. In such instances, nonverbal communication and its understanding have been packaged in such a way as to make people believe it can be used to control others. However, if we come across in any way as seeking to control a person who comes to us for care, we will never stand with him on his "holy ground."

We encourage a commonsense approach to nonverbal communication. Take note of the person's body while you are listening to his or her voice. Listen both to *what* is being said as well as to *how* it is being said. Look at the face. Do the expressions match the person's verbal message, or is something awry? How about the general carriage of the individual? Is she tense? Does he look relaxed? How do emotions affect the way a person speaks? Is the person slurring the words, speaking very rapidly or lethargically? What is the tone in the person's voice? Is it edgy, sad or angry? What is it like to be in the room with this person? Does it feel heavy, distant or engaged?

All of these things can help bridge the gap between the spoken words and the total content of the message. Sometimes it is easy to do and sometimes it is a bit more elusive and difficult to track, but in either case, it is worth spending the energy.

Some nonverbal cues are easy to spot and bring to the person's attention. If someone is very happy in her demeanor while she is saying that she is really down, it is easy to note and comment on. "Gee, you say you're down, but you're smiling and your voice sounds pretty bubbly!" Or take an incident we have no doubt all encountered. A person indicates he or she is not angry verbally, but a flushed face seems to say otherwise. "Well, I know you say it doesn't trouble you, but your face is red and you do seem upset." To the above statement the person may respond, "Well, it gets me angry when people say I'm getting upset; if I wasn't upset before, it gets me going." To that it is sometimes good to follow up by saying, "How come people get to you in that way? There must be a reason."

In many instances, though, the nonverbal cues are a bit more subtle. When this is so, there is a danger of missing them. Consequently, as active listeners, we must try to absorb the verbal message and also try to keep alert to body signs and changes.

Missing the signs, particularly when they are subtle, is not the only danger. Misinterpreting them is another. For example, when we see an expression on someone's face, it is often hard to interpret what is going on in his or her mind. In these instances, it would be a mistake to make someone else's nonverbal sign fit our own interpretation. Not only might we be mistaken, but also the person hearing our guess may become angry or resistant (and with good reason), or may actually agree with us even though our guess was wrong.

When they are vulnerable, many people will agree with our opinion even if they do not really believe what was said. They go along with us for a number of reasons. They may fear rejection, or they may be confused and see agreeing as a way out or possibly as a way to avoid looking into themselves for the answer. Whatever the reason, though, premature interpretation is unnecessary and usually harmful. At the very least, it is not helpful. Moreover, remember that when we do this we are asking them to go along with our "savior complex"—for we are trying to show that we can read their minds.

So, what do you do with a questionable nonverbal cue? The most neutral way of communicating our observation is just to point out the nonverbal sign and ask them what it means. In this way, the door is being opened. They are being asked to take the responsibility to help look at the meaning behind it.

For instance, if a man is reporting how happy he is about getting a new job, but there seems to be a hesitancy in his voice or a flicker of some kind of expression that does not match the mood exactly, this could be pointed out. "You seem really happy, but there is a sound in your voice (or you just had an expression on your face) that...." (The comment is left unfinished on purpose to see what happens.)

To this statement the person may respond in a number of ways:

"Well, it's funny you should pick it up, but I am concerned about the duties in the new job even if it is a promotion I've always wanted."
Or, *"You mean you think I'm not totally happy about the job?"*
Or, *"I'm not sure what you're referring to...."*

If the person answers in the first way nothing more need be done. In the second and third responses, something additional needs to be said to prompt further examination of the nonverbal sign. So the following noncommittal comment might be added: "When you were talking about some of the job's duties, your voice sounded different (or you had this look on your face). I don't have any idea what it meant, but it did confuse me and I wondered what you were thinking."

This further push might get the person to examine the cause for the nonverbal sign. If this happens, fine. If he still seems unwilling or unable to talk about it, just drop the topic and make no more of it. This will leave him with a possible doubt, but not with the pressure of our interpretation to contend with. It is his "sacred ground," and he has the right to explore it or not.

One interesting thing might also happen. Later on, if elements do come up that do not fit exactly with what the person has been saying (if, say, the person does discover a doubt about a decision that seemed completely sound), he may come back to the time when you pointed out the nonverbal sign. Then a clarification of what might have been going on at the earlier time may be broached.

Evaluating Our Reactions

Awareness of our nonverbals. When a person comes to us for care and we are attracted to her burning issue, one of the ways in which we stay with her on her "holy ground" and not push away (or be pushed away) is to be sensitive to our own reactions in the situation. This may sound unusual since our primary concern is to understand her "ground" in the ways mentioned above. However, our own reactions to the situation will give us important cues and our sensitivity to these cues will often determine the depth to which the conversation will go.

This does not mean that the conversation shifts to focus on us. The focus is still on the person who comes with a burning issue. But like Moses, who had to take his shoes off to approach the burning bush, a part of us is exposed in the process of standing on "holy ground." Our task is to evaluate what is going on in us so that it does not get in the way of our attending to the other person. Even more, we need to evaluate what is going on within us to gain additional clues to the nature of the "holy ground" on which we stand in any given moment. Just as scientists have found in quantum mechanics that the act of observation affects the waves and particles in such a way that one cannot observe the wave or particle in itself but only in relationship to the observer,[3] so our own reactions will often affect the interaction between speaker and listener. Our sensitivity to this makes it more possible to stay with a person on that "holy ground."

To begin with, we will want to evaluate our own nonverbal communications. Even the most experienced, caring listener tends to forget that just as the listener can be a sharp observer, so also can the person asking for help. The person asking for help may be extremely sensitive to how he or she is being received. So it is very necessary for us to be aware of the nonverbal communications we send, whether they be blatant or almost imperceptible. This awareness is especially important so we can better judge how our own expressions might affect the interaction.

An illustration of this is when one of us (RJW) first began interviewing as a profession. It was in a criminal justice setting, and my job was to conduct intake interviews in a jail. This entailed trying to get basic information on a new confinee's background, crime and personality so we could ensure they would be placed in the proper program within the institution.

On one particular morning, a young, slightly built sixteen-year-old was led to me. I asked him to sit down and began asking him a number of questions. (My goal at this point in my interviewing career was to fill in the blanks on the form the prison administration gave me. As is the case with many insecure, new interviewers, I was more interested in data than in people and their feelings.) When I reached the section of the questionnaire devoted to a description of the crime (without having had any snags in the interaction to this point), I casually asked, "How come you're in jail?" When he replied, "I shot my grandmother," I gave him a facial expression that said unequivocally, "You did what!!!" In effect, nonverbally I was telling him, "I could understand how you might assault your brother, fight with your mother or rob your father, but nobody, *nobody* shoots their grandmother!"

This blatant early rejection of him naturally did not go unnoticed. From that point on in the session, he became quiet and his answers were brief. After several minutes I realized the impact of my judgmental reaction. If any progress was to be made, I would have to do something to correct my mistake. I decided to confront the issue directly.

"When you mentioned you shot your grandmother earlier, it surprised me and I reacted without thinking. I imagine other people have responded similarly, but that's no excuse. You see, I—possibly like others—didn't stop to hear what you had to say about how this came about. I cut you off. How did you feel when I did that?"

The youth spent several minutes speaking about how he met the same response in others who had prejudged him and that it made him angry and sad. When he completed describing his response, I went on to say, "Well, if I responded to you like everyone else, it's no wonder you wouldn't want to give me a fuller picture of what happened. What did happen anyway?"

At that juncture, I was lucky. He had aired enough of his feelings. He also seemed to feel that, although I was initially prejudiced in my view, I was earnestly interested in hearing his side to the story. So, with my question, he was prompted to continue and we made some progress. The lines of communication were reopened.

The mistakes we make as listeners are not always so blatant (thank goodness!). Likewise, sometimes it is not possible to correct it at the time. The important factor, though, is that we keep aware of as much of our nonverbal communication as possible. The more we are in touch with how we are coming across, the greater our chances are of knowing how we really feel about certain topics. If we tend to be more expressive—either positively or negatively—the probability is that we have some strong feelings in this area. And if we can become alert to these nonverbal expressions, we can work better to deal with the emotions and concerns they represent. For example, suppose when someone speaks of drugs, sex or family violence, it produces strong reactions that are, naturally, facially expressed. In such a case, it would be hard to seem objective when listening to someone discuss problems touching on one of these issues.

Monitoring our own nonverbal communications can be an invaluable asset in helping us learn about ourselves as we work to help others. It makes us aware of our own feelings. It lets us know when we have inadvertently or purposefully sent a message that we feel a certain way about what the other is telling us. And it helps us to control the way we come across when we want to hear someone out without imposing our biases upon him while he is relating his position or plight.

Criticizing our biases. Since our personality provides us with a special way of viewing the external world, we must be careful not to perceive things within too narrow a framework. If we are too narrow-minded, our biases may cause us to misinterpret information, or miss data on the one hand and exaggerate it on the other.

To correct our biases, we must be our own devil's advocate. We must have the courage to critique our own decisions immediately after they are formed. This will serve to relax the rigid channels we sometimes follow when taking in information and judging it.

One way to check our thinking is to take a position opposite to the one we have reached and try to support that opposite position reasonably and thoughtfully. While it probably will not cause us to change our overall impression, in many instances it might help us see some things in a slightly different light. At the very least, it will put us in a good position to liberalize our thinking and uncover our prejudices.

Our prejudices have not been reasoned into us. Therefore, they cannot be reasoned out. The only thing we can do about them is to attempt to be alert and try to uncover them at every turn. Then once we spot them, we should try to deal with them in an open fashion.

People cannot help being prejudiced in some way. Our likes and dislikes have been programmed into us at the preverbal and preschool ages. Our tastes have been long in the making, and as we get older the sources and extent of them multiply. We are not referring to prejudice only in the narrow sense of racial prejudice. What we are talking about is the broad range of unconscious, usually unobtrusive, but insupportable likes and dislikes we have.

In trying to understand a person, elicit data, and work with him or her, prejudice can have a negative impact both in obvious and in subtle ways. It may be as simple as, "He reminds me of my cousin Steve, and boy do I *dislike* my cousin Steve." Or, it could be more subtle. "I met a woman named Carol today, and even before she spoke I knew I was going to like her."

Although the effects of negative bias have been widely publicized, the impact of positive prejudice has not received such attention. Yet positive bias can interfere as much when listening to someone as can its negative counterpart. Good feelings toward someone *can* be a hindrance. That it is easier to work with someone who is likeable is not a dispute. But the fact is that just as we miss important information when we become angry, we can also miss certain elements when we feel very favorably toward the other person.

Consequently, when working with someone we feel very positively toward, we still need to be a devil's advocate in regards to our reactions. For example, if a close friend who is an easy-going, pleasant person tells us of a number of incidences in which her husband humiliated her, it is natural to side with her. No one likes to see a nice person taken advantage of by someone else. Still we must say to ourselves, "Now that I feel she is being exploited and humiliated by her horrible husband, let me ask the question of myself, 'What if I'm all wrong and she is the culprit?' " While this question by itself may seem foolish, it may open the door to new information. It will prevent us from totally blaming the husband and aid us in examining more fully the participating role of the wife.

Asking the woman, "Why does he do it to you?" or "Why do you let him do it to you?" will probably lead to a nonproductive answer such as, "I don't know. I just don't know." By focusing on the part the apparently innocent woman plays, however, some light may be shed on how the interactions between husband and wife foster this behavior. By picturing the wife in an exaggerated role, in complete opposition to our feeling that her husband is a cad, questions that may prove more useful might come to mind, such as those that focus on the woman's active role in the problem.

Some of these questions might be as follows: "Under what circumstances does he react hostilely? How do you react when he treats you this way? What prompts you to handle the situation in the way you do? How often does this happen? What's changed in your relationship? When did it change?"

When we feel warmly toward someone, it is very hard for us to believe that it takes two to tango. However, problems usually arise *between* people and depend on the interaction between people, so it is the relationship that must be focused on, not the merits or faults of isolated "heroes" and "cads."

Anyone can side with a friend, but a caring listener can be even more valuable if she or he aids a friend to see more clearly what is happening. If a person can begin to see how his behavior is making the situation worse, or can view the twisted kind of advantage he enjoys by maintaining the status quo, then the results can be most startling.

In the above situation, for example, we may find out the ways in which the wife encourages verbal battles. We may also uncover the "advantage" of her continuing with such a relationship: "We never seem to talk anymore—the only time I can get his attention is when we argue." This is not a healthy or positive reason for arguing and allowing oneself to be humiliated. Yet a need for attention in a deteriorating and lonely marriage may be the impetus behind this woman's behavior. Such situations are sad, especially since her behavior does not permit this woman to change or grow. If we did not evaluate our reactions and criticize our biases—positive and negative—we might not stand on the "holy ground" of this woman's life where she faces the truth about her marriage and where she hears a call for personal growth.

Evaluating our reactions to distortions and defensive styles. Each of us has learned a way of "dancing" in life; a way of interacting with persons that often repeats itself with everyone with whom we attempt to be close. Often our way of "dancing" in life leads us away from intimate, vulnerable moments. Often we "dance" right off the "holy dance floor" when we come close to it. Look at Moses. After finding himself on holy ground and hearing the Lord speak, he tried every way possible to dance away from what he heard. He made excuses about how the people would react to him. He said he was not an eloquent speaker.

He tried to get Aaron to take his place (Exodus 4). But the Lord would not buy Moses' "dance" and kept him on the dance floor.

We will often find ourselves caught up in the repetitive "dance" of the person who comes to us for care. If we are not attentive, her "dance" will take us right off the "holy dance floor."

Her repetitive "dance" will often be seen in her distorted perception of us as listeners. Quite often a person will emphasize a particular view of us because of the problem she is experiencing. If the person is troubled by finances, for example, as the helper we may be cast as financially well off even though we are in the same league as far as expenses and resources go. If the person is quite depressed, we may be seen as happy-go-lucky and secure. If she is having difficulty in personal relations, she will distort your ability to interact with others. If it is a younger person, you may be told you never had these problems. Or the very reason why she is talking to you ("You have such a happy marriage.") will often turn out to be the reason she believes that you cannot help her ("What would you know about marriage problems?").

At other times a person may react to us the way he has reacted to significant persons in his past. If he is used to getting his needs met through flattery, tears, anger or manipulation, he will do the same with us. And he will expect us to react exactly the way people have reacted to him in the past. Sometimes we fall into his "dance," and it usually takes us off the "holy dance floor." Sometimes we refuse to dance his "dance," and we bear the brunt of his intense emotions.

We must be aware of the distortions of ourselves as listeners if we are to stay on the "holy dance floor." People seeking our help will alternately praise us or condemn us depending upon how they feel rather than as a result of who we really are. In therapy, such projections on the part of clients are dealt with very carefully. In listening to family and friends, it is best to take inflated compliments and deflating put-downs with a block, not just a grain, of salt.

A person's "defensive style" is also a part of his/her way of "dancing" in life. Feelings of anxiety or conflict in times of crisis produce in each of us a way of behaving. Some of us get nervous and defensive; some put up a front that "all is well"; others wish they could just fall apart and let someone else handle it. Recognizing the basic way a person is reacting in a crisis or under stress—recognizing his or her defensive style—is a great advantage in helping that person deal with whatever is at issue. If we recognize their defensive styles, we will not allow them to push us away or collude with them in unhelpful approaches, both of which lead us off the "holy dance floor" and away from the most important of life's issues.

While there are many ways people defend themselves, let us look at five typical styles that we often encounter: false courage or denial, childlike behavior, hostility, depression and evasion.

1. False courage or denial. False courage is one of the most common styles of dealing with stress. This "macho," "stiff-upper-lip" approach is frequently used by people uncomfortable with facing any personal feelings of inadequacy.

"Keeping a stiff upper lip" is often defended in western society, the belief being that we should prevent expressions of emotion and fight dependency at all cost. We also mistakenly equate being unemotional with being strong and in control.

The kernel of truth in this myth is that self-control in a crisis is better than falling apart. However, while self-control is essential for effective action, it does not preclude admitting one's predicament or temporarily leaning on someone. But the person using false courage does not admit this. Instead, he finds facing a problem so repugnant that he consciously or unconsciously suppresses the severity of the problem. Frequently such an individual will even go a step further and act in a way directly opposite to the weakness he feels (in mental health jargon, this is referred to as "reaction formation").

The incongruities that result are usually obvious to everyone but the person involved. A student failing his senior year in high school may be filling out applications for Harvard and Yale. An aerospace engineer slated to lose her job may be spending money like she is getting a promotion next week. A man who is having problems in his marriage may be describing it in glowing terms to his closest friends.

Due to the massive denial and great fear of appearing weak,

this type of person is very difficult to deal with effectively. In most cases, the best thing one can do is provide general support and point out some of the incongruities in as nonthreatening a way as possible. (For example, "You have come to me for care, but as you talk about this it seems like you have no problem.") Confrontation accomplishes little, if anything, with this kind of individual.

With the failing student who is applying to Harvard, there would be little point in criticizing his choice or removing his fantasy. Instead, something might be achieved by discussing with him how he plans to raise his failing grades so he does not miss fall enrollment. In addition, when he gives this information and it is explored as much as he permits, then some attention can be given to how he could be hedging his bets by applying to other colleges, a practice employed by all good students.

What we are trying to do with this type of person is to provide support for her and show faith in her problem-solving abilities. We are also trying to stay on the "holy dance floor" with her and not get led astray by her false impression of being in control. We can miss the "sacred territory" by either being too confrontational or by colluding with her presentation that there is no problem.

Take, for example, the case of the man heartily describing his marriage, while suppressing the difficulties in it:

"Oh, Alice couldn't be better! She's a great gal. Starting her own business, too!"
"Oh, that sounds exciting."
"Yeah, I'm all for it. Gets her out of the house, you know. It's something she's always wanted. I'm all for it."
"You look a little down in the mouth when you say that, though...."

Depending upon his response to your remark, his feelings on the matter can then be explored as far as he permits.

2. Childlike behavior. Childlike behavior is another defensive style commonly displayed by people under stress. This kind of person seems immobilized by problems. In a pleading voice he asks, "What am I going to do?" Anxiety, conflict and frustration push him to regress to a temporary, dependent role. He wants to be parented, hugged and led around—though often he seems to resist and fight your directive efforts if you try to be mother or father to him.

This kind of style can be quite annoying. The temptation for some of us is to say, "Snap out of it!" Telling this type of individual to shape up or ship out usually accomplishes little. At most he may be temporarily pushed to action, but this action will soon cease, and we will find that we have missed an opportunity to stay on the "holy dance floor" with him.

One of the most effective ways of handling this type of individual is to behave toward him in a manner that indicates your faith in the person's ability to deal with the situation competently. Your behavior should seem to say, "You're independent and have resources. You can handle it."

Now there is a big difference between *saying* this to a person and *modeling* the message through your behavior. In saying the words, the result is often an ineffective pep talk that will leave you, the listener, quite frustrated. Modeling the message is done through interacting with the person in a way that demonstrates your belief in his ability to get himself and the situation together. This conveys a sense of trust that we spoke of earlier. Demonstrate your faith not by giving advice, but by being quiet and nondirective, asking him what he feels and thinks he should do. This keeps us on the "holy dance floor" and keeps us from colluding in keeping him dependent.

> *"I just don't know what to do. What should I do? What would you do in my place?"*
>
> *"Well, what do you think you should do?"*
>
> *"I don't know. What do you think?"*
>
> *"Well, there must be something you would like to do."*
>
> *"There are things I know I should do, but I can't."*
>
> *"What do you think you should do then?"*
>
> *"I should forget the marriage and divorce him."*
>
> *"What makes you think you should do that?"*
>
> *"Well, it seems like my only choice, so I have to do it."*
>
> *"You could do it, but think out loud about the other options you might have."*

"Do you think there are other options? What do you think they would be?"

"You're in the situation and know yourself and your husband better than I. I'd be interested in hearing you bring up some of the alternatives open to you, other than breaking up with him."

In the above conversation the listener is trying to show the person that some of the difficulty in making a decision is in seeing only one dramatic solution. Maybe there is only one solution, but other options need to be entertained first. The listener is also trying to keep the focus and problem-solving responsibility on the dependent person. As can be seen, it is often not easy. But jumping in and rescuing this person accomplishes little and, in fact, leads us off the "holy dance floor" where he or she has to struggle with the problem and seek revelation about how to proceed.

3. Hostility. Hostility also rears its head when certain kinds of individuals are under stress and seeking help. After dropping hints about their present problems, they show hostility or at least suspicion when someone attempts to intervene. Like the bravado of those who display false courage, these individuals are worried about being vulnerable. This gnawing fear is, "If they see I'm not doing so well, what will they think of me? And how will they then treat (exploit) me?"

Due to this fear, they strike out first through hostility. Their thinking is, "Get them first, since they will take advantage of me if they have a chance," or, "I know that anger will push them away from my sensitive area so they cannot see it." The result is that people shy away from them, which supports their original fear that people are not *really* interested in them. These are the kinds of people we are constantly avoiding or making the statement to them, "Now, don't be like that. I'm only trying to help."

Hostility may also take the form of displaced anger. While they are with the causes of their difficulties, they are quiet. Then they come into contact with someone who is nice to them and—bang!—the anger gets redirected from the original target onto them. This is when most of us quietly leave the "sacred dance floor" and do not stay around to find out what is really going on.

No one enjoys taking a verbal thrashing from a friend or from someone who has asked us to care, but if we realize where the anger is really directed, we can point it out. Also, we can simply comment on her anger and get her to say more, conveying a sense of trust that we can handle her anger. Further, by recognizing that the person's hostility is due to anxiety, it is a bit easier not to feel so personally affected by her comments.

4. Depression. A fourth way of reacting to problems is depression. This reaction is familiar to all of us. In fact, depression is so common that it will be given separate treatment in chapter 7. For now, though, it will be enough to emphasize that dealing with the depressive style of handling problems requires patience and detachment on the part of the listener.

Depressive persons can drag you down with them if you are not alert to this basic principle: *You cannot help depressed people over a period of time if you join in their sadness or if you expect them to improve too quickly.*

This is more easily said than done. In our efforts to be empathetic, getting caught up with the person's helplessness and hopelessness is quite easy. Likewise, in our action-oriented society, trying to get a lethargic, emotionally depressed person to start moving again is a natural goal. In the first instance, he is dragging us off the "holy dance floor," and in the second instance, we are dragging him off.

Motivating a depressed individual is not easy. Hope must be held out for him or her. Yet improvement must be seen in terms of slow progress over time. Both the one listening and the one asking for care must have patience with a seeming lack of forward movement.

5. Evasion. The final style of reacting to stress or problems in life is evasion. Evasion is a blocking out of information from our conscious thoughts, and it is a common manner of handling difficult situations. We frequently employ evasion when we avoid potentially disturbing situations and when we try to ignore existing problems in our lives.

For instance, we occasionally try to avoid hearing bad news. We shut off the TV as they are about to report on starvation in a poor country. We quickly turn the page of the paper rather than read a story of a rape incident. We do this because such news disturbs us. For any number of reasons we would rather avoid these stories. For us these problems do not exist for the moment. We are determined to put them out of our minds.

Evasiveness can also take the form of avoiding an existing personal problem, rather than dealing directly with it. When people bring the problem up, some of us give brief, simplified answers and change the subject. Other people will joke about it rather than deal with an uncomfortable issue. Still others just ignore what is being said.

Various messages are being sent by us and other people when we do this. One of them is, "Leave me alone. It's too overwhelming at this point. Let someone else take the responsibility for handling it because I surely am not ready to do it."

When therapists deal with massive blocking on the part of patients who are extremely disturbed, they move very slowly at opening up these areas. However, in dealing with someone who is basically healthy and just seems to desire to avoid an issue, it can be handled more actively.

One way this can be done is by pointing to the fact that the person is avoiding a topic and indicating that you appreciate that the topic must be upsetting to her. If someone says, "I don't want to talk about it!" you can at least indicate, "Well, you must be pretty upset if you don't want to talk about it." If this, too, meets with a refusal to discuss it, then it might be best to say one additional thing. "Well, if you don't want to talk about it now, it's OK, but you'll have to talk about it with someone sometime if it's ever going to get resolved."

Some people think it is best not to pursue an issue if someone is evasive or openly refuses to talk about it. This is not necessarily the best route. When someone refuses to discuss a matter, remaining silent is tantamount to agreeing that the subject must indeed be so unapproachable that he is right in not wanting to talk about it or, worse yet, in not wanting to face it.

Reinforcing such positions is incorrect. This does not mean that we should push, push, push. As indicated above, we should not agree with her premise, but instead, give her the feeling that it is all right if she wants to *postpone* talking about it. In this way, we respect her right to silence while disagreeing with her fear of facing the supposedly terrible issue.

The major defensive styles covered here are not the only ones people use when dealing with life problems, and they should not be seen as mutually exclusive. The hostile person, for example, may also exhibit childish behavior.

In discussing these defenses, the goal is not to point out pathological styles but merely to indicate that people respond in different ways when they are boxed in by their own frustrations or environments. To understand these styles, even at a very elementary level, is to better appreciate the person and the problem. In recognizing how a person is acting, we can better intervene with him as well. We will not so easily be led off the "holy dance floor," but will stay to stand on that "holy ground" and see what will be revealed. A hostile person will not push us away. We will not collude with an evasive person in avoiding important topics. We will be better able to maintain a helpful stance toward the depressed person rather than getting dragged down or frustrated by him.

Robert Kegan has said that, "Our survival and development depend on our capacity to recruit the invested attention of others to us."[4] He goes on to say that not only must we attract someone to us, but someone must *stay* if healthy development is to occur. The burning problems in a person's life may attract us like the burning bush attracted Moses. But will we stay to stand on "holy ground"? Whether we choose to stay or whether someone allows us to stay depends on a creative mix of conveying trust, understanding their "ground," not being led astray by their defensive style and being aware of our own reactions to them. It is like a "dance on holy ground" that can be transforming, and the Lord dances with us. Or as the contemporary song set to a Shaker melody says,

> "Dance then wherever you may be;
> 'I am the Lord of the dance,' said he,
> 'And I'll lead you all, wherever you may be,
> And I'll lead you all in the dance,' said he."[5]

4. Intentional Caring: Conversation with a Goal

When a person comes to us for care, if we are to be of any help our conversation must be more than ordinary, everyday conversation. Everyday conversation is free-floating, usually aimless, and entered into quite naturally by most of us. Everyday conversation has ill-defined goals that can quickly change. Everyday conversation is easy but not always productive. We cannot count on discovering things during everyday conversation; we might, but unless we are on our toes and making an effort to elicit certain material during the encounter, nothing is guaranteed.

A professional therapist will actually conduct an interview that is a purposeful conversation with the goal of securing information. In initial interviews the professional is purposefully attempting to uncover the real issues and to make a diagnosis. Even for the professional, it is important in a successful interview not to be rigid and authoritarian or use a "professional voice." It is important to be relaxed and to put the client at ease.

When a person comes to us for care we will not be conducting a formal diagnostic interview, but, nonetheless, our conversation should be purposeful and we should try to maintain a relaxed, personal atmosphere. We should be purposeful, yet avoid "playing parent" and treating the person in trouble like a child. Treating the person as an adult and viewing his or her problem with respect will encourage the expression of feelings and the discovery of what is truly happening in a person's life.

This may seem like a difficult undertaking, but it does not

have to be. If several things are kept in mind, a purposeful conversation can go quite smoothly. Here are some basic pointers:

1. Try to put yourself in the other person's position. How would you like a neighbor or friend to address you if you had a problem?

2. Active listening and reasonable questioning procedures—not probing—will get you the information you need.

3. Do not treat a person seeking help like a child, because that will greatly inhibit the person's problem-solving abilities. In times of trouble, it is the adult part of the person you are appealing to and are trying to help him rediscover.

4. Remember that humility is a valuable asset. Humility is knowing what is good about yourself, knowing those aspects of yourself that are not always desirable and accepting both groups of character traits as reality. Humility is essential for working with people because it is easy to lose sight of the reality about ourselves and unthinkingly impose ourselves on others.

Jesus and Purposeful Conversation

Jesus did not conduct formal diagnostic interviews of persons who came to him, but he did use conversation with a goal. For instance, his conversation with the Samaritan woman at the well was not everyday conversation (John 4:7–30). Jesus engaged the Samaritan woman in conversation with a simple request for some water. Even that simple request alerted the woman to the uniqueness of this moment, since it was not normal for a Jew to speak to a Samaritan woman.

Quickly and easily Jesus moves the conversation to a deeper level, keeping the focus on the woman and beginning to tease out spiritual issues in her life that she did not want to see. He begins to talk about "living water," and it begins to emerge that she is a person whose life is missing something which could not be found in five husbands, nor in a current lover. They talk about the unspeakable portion of her life, and Jesus treats the woman with respect and without judgment. She sees what she has never seen before, and her own gifts are mobilized as she goes to tell others about what she has seen.

This is relaxed conversation, but it is not aimless conversation. It is conversation with a goal, based upon Jesus' understanding of the human condition in general and his perception of the unique needs of this woman in particular.

Intentional Caring but Not Psychotherapy

When our caring is intentional, we will use conversation with a goal. Conversation that is goal-oriented is based on assumptions of what we see as important. When our conversation is purposeful, we make some assumptions about human nature, the purpose of life and our own limited roles as listeners. Our assumptions shape what we do. We have certain objectives in mind as we listen, question and interpret. Our caring is more effective when we are clear about our assumptions.

One of the assumptions we make is that goal-oriented conversation is not the same thing as intensive psychotherapy. Therapy's aim is often personality change. It is an in-depth process requiring specific and extensive education and expertise. Therapy can take considerable time since it usually deals with problems that can be quite severe.

The object of intentional caring is not to change the personality of a person, give advice nor solve a person's problem for him/her. Instead the goal is, at least in part, to open up the means for the person to do his or her own problem-solving with resources that are already present. When Jesus encounters the woman at the well, he builds upon her knowledge of water, of tradition, of God and of the Messiah, helping her to see these in a new light. This new light creates alternatives for her life, moving her from someone who is trapped in the drudgery of daily work and failed relationships to a person with a higher purpose and meaning in life.

Purposeful conversation guides the process of exploration and discovery where a situation is examined, resources identified and alternatives clarified. The person will do his own decision-making and problem-solving. The caregiver simply helps him or her uncover the means to do so. This is done by (1) reflecting the person's emotions, (2) focusing on the person's assets as well as limitations, (3) helping the person clarify the issues and behaviors involved and (4) helping the person identify and evaluate alternatives.

Exploring feelings. Intentional caring will make persons aware of their own feelings about issues or people they discuss. This is an important undertaking because, where emotions are strong, they will surely affect the person's actions and opinions.

Anger, disgust, elation, love, hate, warmth, fear, annoyance—these feelings can alter a perception in such a way that the person becomes mired in distortion. There is nothing intrinsically wrong with emotions. But when they are so exaggerated that they prevent someone from taking personal control, or when a person is so unaware of their presence that their influence on the situation is ignored, then they inhibit the person's problem-solving ability and are an unwanted interference.

Thus, reflecting and exploring emotions are important parts of conversation with a goal. It permits the person to open up, to identify and evaluate the feelings he has. The fascinating thing about reflecting a person's emotions is the complexity it unearths regarding the ways people feel about things. While most of us single out one emotion to describe our reaction to an event, we actually feel an array of them.

For instance, many people may describe how angry they are but smile as they report the incident. Others say they feel confident about something, but their eyes say otherwise. These things have to be pointed out to the person. If they are not, the ambivalence they feel will be missed (see chapter 3 and the discussion of nonverbals).

Feelings also need to be defined. More and more, we are finding that getting people to elaborate on the feelings they claim is extremely useful. They get to see in greater detail the many aspects and ramifications of their reported emotions.

"I'm quite annoyed over the way my boss handled the situation. There I am in front of several of the people who work for me, and he reads me the riot act."

"You're annoyed?"

"Yeah, he has got to be kidding. (Voice is getting louder; face is starting to tighten up.) What are they going to think of me now? Who does he think he is anyway?"

"You say you're annoyed, but you seem more angry than merely annoyed."

"I guess I am. I really looked bad."

"It must make you angry looking so bad in front of your subordinates."

"You're not kidding! What are they going to think of me?"

"After that episode, you sound a bit concerned about the way your people are going to see you."

"I am concerned. Suppose they start feeling, 'Well, he's a real loser; look how the boss treats him.' It bothers me." (Starting to sound quite down about the situation.)

"It really does bother you, doesn't it?"

"It really does."

"This thing seems to have you really down."

"Boy, it does. I get worried when someone does something like that to me."

"What worries you about that kind of treatment? It sounds like it's happened to you before."

In the above illustration, the depth of emotions was explored. What was described at first as annoying was actually very upsetting. What initially appeared to be concern revealed a pattern of worry that might lead to depression. The emotions turned out to be more serious than initially reported. If the initial reports were accepted and not questioned, we would never have understood how this person really felt or the true scope of the underlying problem.

In reflecting people's emotions, we use *their* words, or synonyms for them, to get them to talk further about how they feel. We should also key in on nonverbal signs and observe what they indicate about others' feelings (see chapter 3). Then, together we can examine all of these indicators.

One positive result of reflecting a person's feelings, aside from getting an idea of the actual feelings involved and the scope of the problem, is the catharsis experienced by the person seeking help. When people are able to get in touch with their feelings, one of the benefits is that they get a chance to let off steam. The result can be amazingly therapeutic. They start off a conversation feeling tense and jittery. We might think we accomplished little with them. Yet they leave us noticeably more relaxed and thankful for our help saying, "I feel so much better. Thanks for your help," or, "Gee, that's a load off my chest. I appreciate your listening. You always were a good friend."

As people unload their troubles, the burden becomes lighter. They get a chance to look at what is going on and how they feel about it. In addition, they are able eventually to achieve some objectivity toward the issues when they are out in the open. This objectivity would not have been possible before, given the tension they were experiencing.

A potential hazard of reflecting a person's emotions is that it can lead to a dead end. When this happens, breaking the circle is easy—and essential.

> *"It seems you feel down."*
> *"Yes, I really feel blue."*
> *"Boy, you do seem blue."*
> *"Yes. I am depressed."*
> *"You certainly seem depressed."*

This kind of encounter is not getting anywhere. The person has already expressed that he or she is not feeling up to par. The caregiver has reflected the feeling a number of times. If this continued, it would be natural for the client to say, "Well, we've established that I'm depressed, blue and down. Now what?"

Without belittling the reflection process, which is essential to get the client to open up and recognize the caregiver's empathy for the feelings involved, reflection cannot be used alone. Once an emotion is expressed in full, more details are necessary. Namely, *when* did the person become depressed (or more depressed than normal)? Under *what circumstances* did he or she become depressed? With *whom* does he/she react this way? And, if necessary, *when* has this emotion occurred *in the past?* (This is done to elucidate a pattern of situations that produce the reaction. It is not conducted as a psychoanalytic safari into the hidden past.)

Reflection of emotions is an essential aim of intentional caring. It helps persons needing care to get in touch with their real feelings, and it helps the caregiver better understand other people and their problems. It is a way for us to show them we have a good idea of what they are going through, how they are feeling and what they are experiencing. Only after the process of reflection seems to be going no further do we try to move to questions regarding circumstances.

Focusing on assets. Intentional caring should be a balanced, positive undertaking. It must concern itself not only with a person's limitations, but it must also uncover and emphasize a person's assets. When it does not, progress becomes elusive. Our conversation with a goal may elucidate inappropriate or fruitless patterns of dealing with a situation, but to do so at the expense of opening up and emphasizing the resources a person has to solve the dilemma is a major mistake. If the person walks away feeling, "Yes, it's true; I am really messed up!" then the session has been a failure. As much attention needs to be given to positive abilities as is paid to problematic liabilities.

In the reflection process, we reflect positive feelings ("You seem really happy about this.") as much as we do negative ones. The same should be done in uncovering assets and limitations. Frequently a person's difficulty is simply the "other side of the coin" of a similar positive trait.

For instance, a person who takes criticism too personally may run into problems. People may not want to be around him because they have a fear of offending him. However, in trying to get the person to see this pattern we would not want to ignore the positive value of his sensitivity. This individual may possess a fine ability to be attuned to other people and the world at large. An insecure perception of self may color his concept of how others see him, but in other instances where a personal opinion is not involved, such distortions may not be present. So, in discriminating when sensitivity is a problem, efforts must be made to also note when it is a help.

This is not accomplished by giving the person a pep talk or

by mouthing general remarks that have nothing to do with the situation in question. Comments like, "Look, you're OK. Just don't think about the problem," are too general and ignore the troubles the person is experiencing. When our comments are related to what is actually happening and take into consideration both the person's assets and liabilities, they can be quite helpful.

"What they say about me is upsetting. I guess I'm just too sensitive. I care too much. I guess that's my problem. If I didn't worry about other people's perceptions of me, I'd be in a better place emotionally right now."

"But you do care."

"Yes, I do. I want to come across effectively. I want people to like me. I don't want to be seen as a terrible person."

"Well then, why wouldn't you want to continue to be the type of person who cares about other people's feelings and opinions?"

"Because it hurts too much."

"Does it hurt all of the time, or just when you feel they're saying negative things about you?"

"Oh, it's just when I feel they're putting me down."

"Do people ever give you feedback that they like it when you're sensitive to their needs and feelings?"

"Yes. In fact, people say I'm so considerate of them. They feel I'm tactful. I don't just open my mouth, say what I feel like and hurt them like Maryann. She's someone who lives in the neighborhood. She never seems to have anything nice to say. Nor does she ever know when to keep quiet."

"So your being sensitive to others causes you problems only when the comments are directed to you, or you feel they are?"

"Yes. That's right."

"So, what we need to look at is not your ability to be sensitive to your environment, but when this gets you into trouble in terms of feeling put down by others?"

"Yes. That's right. If I could just figure out why little statements get to me."

"Well, when was the last time someone said something to you that hurt?"

(Person goes on to describe incident, and both she and the counselor look at it together for clues.)

In the above illustration there is an effort to show that the person's sensitivity is not generally bad, but only selectively a problem. In certain instances it is even a plus. Then an illustration is requested. This is done so the person can begin to see the problem not as something mysterious but as something that can be brought into more distinct focus.

Clarifying issues. Intentional caring attempts also to help persons in need to take constructive action on their own behalf. Their ability to do so depends upon uncovering their own problem-solving skills. When people come to us for help, it is often because their problem-solving abilities seem paralyzed. The more they act, the more they see themselves being pulled down into interpersonal quicksand.

"I don't know what to say to her anymore."

"What do you mean?"

"Well, it seems the more I try to discuss her late hours and her running around, the more she resents it. In the past we used to talk about things. She listened to me. Now, when I tell her what I think, she gets angry and storms out. I just don't know what to do. If I can't discuss things with her, what chance do I have of making any kind of impact. I feel so helpless."

When people come in need of care, futility and frustration often darken their outlook and are reflected in their downtrodden carriage and sad facial expression. There seems to be no way out. If there are any alternatives, either they do not see them, or they do not like them. The message they give us is that unless something drastic happens, the situation cannot be solved—at least not by them.

Due to the apparent hopelessness of it all, they seem to want to hear two different things: "Yes, you're right, the situation is hopeless," and, "This is going to be easy because I know the magical solution to the problem." While many people do not really believe either message, they feel that both might somehow be true because they cannot see any alternatives.

This kind of despondency needs to be handled with care. If we start to feel the hopelessness of the person, we may become despondent too. We may also rush around mentally in an effort to come up with a neat new idea to solve the troubles at hand. Neither action is helpful nor rewarding.

What is usually helpful is to reexamine what the person is doing to alleviate the problem. Feeling caught in a frustrating, seemingly hopeless muddle can be the result of the person's not recognizing what he is or is not doing in certain circumstances. Reexamining the person's behavior can help clarify the issues and open up alternatives and possible solutions to the difficulty.

"You say you've discussed the situation with your daughter. It seems to make it worse, and in the past this wasn't the case."

"Yes, that's right."

"Do you perceive any change in the way you discuss things with your daughter over the past year?"

"I'm not sure what you mean."

"Well, has your style changed in how you broach topics with her?"

"No, not that I'm aware of. It's more her changing toward me. In the past she listened to me and followed my instructions. Now she doesn't."

"So, in the past she would hear you out calmly, then take your advice?"

"Calmly? Are you kidding?"

"Ah. She reacted in the past as she reacts now?"

"Yes. She has always had a hot head. Only then I could convince her."

"You mean she would wind up agreeing with you all of the time?"

"No. She rarely felt I was right all of the time. It's just that she was more respectful. I had control over her. She listened to me."

"So, what has changed then is her going along with you?"

"Yes. It seems she doesn't listen anymore."

"And by 'doesn't listen' you mean she hears what you have to say, doesn't agree, and acts according to how she feels concerning the matter."

"That's right."

"Well, I'm not clear then about your feelings that she doesn't hear you out; that she doesn't seem to be open to discussing things with you as in the past."

"If she would sit down and talk things over, she'd see I'm right. You have to be there. I just start telling her and she gets up and storms out. How would you feel?"

"How do you feel when she does that?"

"I get so angry I could smash her. I just don't know what to do."

"How does she feel during these interactions?"

"Who knows?"

"You said that in a voice as if you meant 'who cares.'"

"She gets me so angry. Wouldn't you get angry if your child wouldn't hear you out?"

"It seems, though, that you do care. What gets you angry doesn't appear to be the fact that she storms out as much as that she doesn't follow your advice anymore."

"All of it gets me angry, but I wish she'd listen to me...take my advice. She's going to get herself into a lot of trouble."

"If you could get her to hear you out, you might have a better chance to win her over. However, her staying to listen to you and her taking your advice are two different things, aren't they?"

"Well, I doubt if she'll listen to anything I have to say. She doesn't give me a chance."

"Does she feel you give her a chance?"

"It's funny that you say that. She's always said that I didn't take her feelings into account. But I've always had her best interests at heart. She's still a child. I am her mother."

"Yes, you are. She is nineteen though. In the past when you disagreed, you felt better because in the end she capitulated and followed your directives. Now your arguments seem to end in her doing what she wants and her being angry at you. You also end up being angry and frustrated with her."

"So, we're back to square one. I'm caught."

"Both of you are caught if you try to impose your will on her or if you angrily argue instead of discussing the alternatives."

"So, you think I should pamper her? You think I should let her do what she damn well pleases without objecting if I don't agree?"

"Is that what I said?"

"That's what I heard. You want me to discuss things with her. She'd never hear me out. You know she has a temper. It's not all my fault."

"Well, it's no wonder that you would not want to discuss things if you felt that was the same as agreeing with her, pampering her and letting her do what she pleases. You may also be right that it will be hard to convince her that you just want to be heard out. She may react in an angry way in the beginning, thinking you're just trying to get her to do your bidding through another means. And, by the way, you might be determined to do just that."

"What do you mean?"

"Well, you have strong opinions on right and wrong. Discussion isn't real if you're not going to consider the possibility that you may be wrong. Also, discussion usually has a ground rule that the other person has the right to decide that you're wrong and they're right. Are you willing to play by that ground rule?"

"I know she's not a child, but...."

"You see, when you first came in, you complained that she didn't listen to you; that she wouldn't even discuss her staying out late with you. This may not be the case. She may be willing to at least discuss things with you, but as an adult."

"You mean it's my fault that she's this way?"

"No, I mean if you still want to discuss things with her, it still may be possible to do that. She may listen to you. She may be worried in the beginning that you're just trying a new tactic to win her over. So, at first she may be angry and fearful that in the end you will win out and she'll be treated like a child again. But, if you want to at least get your views heard without arguing, there's reason to believe you still can do it."

"But there's no guarantee she'll listen."

"Is there any guarantee she's listening now?"

"No, that's just it. She's not listening. It's like she hates me."

"Hates you, or hates arguing and being dictated to?"

This fairly lengthy narrative points out a number of caring principles. First, it demonstrates one way of focusing on a person's ability to recognize and change styles of interaction. This is done by uncovering and identifying several separate issues:

1. The daughter is no longer a child, but a young adult with a mind of her own.

2. Arguing and discussing are two different things.

3. What the mother sees as a hopeless situation is not definitely so. The frustration is arising from her unwillingness to try relating to her daughter in a different way. (This was brought out without going into, in any depth, her possible fears of losing control over her daughter, who is now entering adulthood.)

4. The mother sees having an open discussion with her daughter as being tantamount to pampering her child and letting her run wild.

5. Her daughter's love of her and her daughter's willingness to go along 100 percent while being treated as an ignorant, ill-behaved child are two different things. (The mother has probably long equated obedience with love.)

There is more in the interaction, but for our purposes now, the five points above are sufficient. The main emphasis has been to recognize and identify issues and behaviors. People are prevented from using their problem-solving talents when situations become confused. The confusion leads to feelings of frustration and hopelessness. Tempers rise or emotions fall, and the situation seems to be an irretrievable mess.

However, by not getting mixed up in the emotions of the situation, we can calmly point out areas of confusion, emotion, vagueness and strength. It is quite easy to get baited into reacting emotionally to the person having the problem. But we must be careful to stay on our toes and remain calm. If we get upset or frustrated, we will only compound the problem. To point out some of the issues to the person in a calm, straightforward fashion, while exploring the feelings the person has about the issue being discussed, is our main objective in this case.

Opening up alternatives. Once some of the relevant issues and behaviors have been identified and the problem no longer seems such a muddle, it will be easier for the person needing care to see and explore alternative behaviors and solutions. This is where real problem-solving comes in.

Problem-solving centers on opening up alternatives that the person needing care can accept as real for them. When we provide intentional care, we are in the option business, not the brainwashing business, no matter how right we believe we are. Our purpose is not to solve a problem *per se,* but rather to introduce new perspectives and new avenues of approach while accepting and supporting the other person's right to choose his or her own mode of action.

The following interaction explores a problem, clarifies some issues, and leads to the exploration of ways of dealing with the situation.

....*"Well, tell me about your daughter's school problems before the suspension."*

"She's never been a good student."

"What do you mean?"

"Well, she always just got by. We've been in for parent conferences again and again. My husband won't even go anymore."

"How do you feel about that?"

"Well, I guess I can understand his being fed up with it all."

"But how do you feel all in all?"

"Well, to be honest, I'm tired, too. I hate to be the one who's always being called in because Jill isn't measuring up or is smoking in the back of the class. Can't they do anything?"

"So the problem isn't a new one?"

"Not by a long shot. Jill has been a pain in the neck for years as far as school goes."

"And it sounds like you feel you've been bearing the brunt of it and are a bit angry at the school and your husband for not doing their share."

"Not exactly angry. I guess they've done their part."

"Whether they have or not is another story. You've been dealing with this problem for some time, though, and you sound a bit frustrated and angry, which would be natural under the circumstances."

"Well, I hate to admit it, but I guess I am. It gets to me."

"So how did you feel when you were told about the suspension?"

"As I said, I was upset. I could have brained her and the principal as well."

"How did you handle Jill when she came home?"

"I smashed her and sent her to her room. She's lucky I didn't kill her. I was livid."

"Did you say anything to her?"

"I just yelled. I probably told her the same things I usually say:

that she's a problem, I get no peace and that she's ruining my life. And if she wants to do that, it's OK with me."

"How did she react?"

"She started yelling at me that no one understood. She actually told me it was my fault and that the principal was a tight ass and didn't understand either."

"What did you have to do regarding the school?"

"Well, I called the principal. I was angry, but I kept cool because I didn't want them to throw Jill out. She only has six months to graduation. She has to go back next week when her suspension is up. I've lectured her until I'm blue in the face. I don't know what else to do."

"What has the school's reaction been?"

"Well, the teacher says she's unruly and he just can't handle her, but will give it one more try. The principal says she has one more opportunity to prove herself."

"So you feel under the gun with regards to her returning."

"I sure do. My husband says he doesn't give a damn. They sound serious at school. And Jill, if you can believe it, says she's going to try hard."

"You have doubts?"

"She's said that a million times before. Then she's gotten into trouble again."

"You sound like you're beating your head against the wall and getting nowhere."

"Is that ever true. I just don't know what to do next. Her sister was a fine student. She's doing well in college. Her younger brother is loved, I mean really loved by all of his teachers. Then there's Jill. I keep telling her that if she doesn't graduate she'll be stuck with lousy jobs all of her life, but it doesn't sink in."

"You seem to have an investment in keeping her in school, then."

"You're not kidding. Wouldn't you?"

"How about Jill's investment?"

"She's only a child, and not a very intelligent one at that. I'm sure that she'd up and leave given the chance, but I told her that I was going to get her through, no matter what."

"How did she react to that?"

"She told me I was always pushing her."

"Does she feel she's being treated differently than the other children?"

"Yes, she does. She feels I pick on her and not on Larry and Marie. But if I do, it's for her own good and also because they've never given me such problems."

"So she is set apart—even if it is for her own good?"

"Yes. Do you think I'm wrong in doing that?"

"You have her best interests at heart. But there's a difference between that and the results of handling something in a particular way."

"So you think I'm messing it up, don't you?"

"Do you think what you've been doing is helping?"

"No, but I don't know what else to do."

"Well, there seems little else open at this point, but there may be. The important thing to remember is that you are trying to help her, and you're upset because the problem still seems to be present. I guess that's why I get the impression you're willing to try some new strategies with her, and open up possibilities of new goals as well."

"What do you suggest?"

"Nothing other than that we go over the way she views school, you view school, the value your husband sees in it, and the different ways things may turn out and how people would react to them."

The stage is now set for brainstorming, or exploring various approaches to the problem, leaving the possible outcomes open. At this point in the conversation, these factors may be obvious to the caregiver, but not to the one seeking care:

1. Success in school is being pushed by the mother and resisted at some level by the daughter.

2. The daughter is being compared with the other children who are school oriented. Even if she succeeds in getting out of high school, it won't be a real success because the parents will probably respond to the effect that, "Whew, well at least she got out of school. Thank goodness for small favors. Now she's on her own. We did what we could."

3. The mother is oblivious to an alternative such as night high school.

In opening up alternatives, it is not in the best interest of the mother to try to convince her that the above points are true. Neither is it appropriate to try to convince her to act according to our set beliefs. Taking the opposing view that her daughter need not necessarily finish school this June will accomplish nothing. It will only put us on opposite sides of the fence. Furthermore, going too fast and imposing values on the person can only backfire and cause hard feelings.

The only thing we should not shy away from is an evaluation of the effectiveness of how something is handled by the client. If the person takes personal affront, then this must be questioned. For example, when the mother took offense at the suggestion that alternate approaches *might* be more effective, a differentiation was made between the motivation, which was positive, and the results, which were negative. This differentiation is essential because many people have long equated efforts with intentions and will get upset when we question the effectiveness of their behavior, if they mistakenly assume that we are questioning their intentions.

In the case now under discussion, the goals should be to make the daughter's, mother's and other significant persons' aims explicit. Then the need is to look at other possible outcomes, such as Jill's getting thrown out of school, Jill's leaving school and taking a job or Jill's going to school at night.

As these areas are explored, if the person balks at discussing them, this must be brought to the forefront in a non-threatening manner.

"There's no sense in discussing other alternatives. Jill is going to stay in school and that's that."

"Well, if you feel that's the only option, I can understand how upset you are—considering the possibility that other things might occur."

If the person is not willing to look at alternatives to continuing in school on a full-time, day-school basis, at least you can look at ways in which the mother can take the sting out of the daughter having to stay in school and out of trouble.

In discovering ways to lighten the burden on the daughter,

it may be helpful to get the daughter's views via the mother. This can be done by asking the mother to relate the kinds of comments—positive, negative or otherwise—made by the daughter in response to the issue of her continuing in school. Any number of things may be uncovered:

1. The daughter may feel that no one says anything to her if school goes well, but if she messes up, they punish her.

2. No one expresses interest in her day other than to say, "How did school go today, Hon? Fine? Oh, that's good."

3. No one gives her future—possibly in a trade or in a clerical position—as much support and positive reinforcement as they give her siblings, who are in college and looking for a "profession."

4. People express surprise when she does well and nod knowingly when she fails.

Bringing these things out in the open can help the person arrive at feasible solutions in conjunction with the counselor.

It is essential to understand that real change takes time and planning. And planning takes specifics. Only after the specifics of the situation are made clear can someone try to implement a new approach or try out new behavior. This may require some role playing with the caregiver to see how similar situations might be handled differently. Then the new behavior may need to be tried out with people other than the significant persons who represent the eventual targets of this new mode of acting.

For instance, a planned new approach may start out with a simple question by the counselor to consider how something might be handled differently: "Well, Sue, if you had to do it again, how would you deal with Elyse in this situation?"

Once this question is answered, the same situation could be approached from different angles: "OK, so you feel you would have liked to do____. What's another way you might have handled it?"

Once two or more approaches have been discussed, the old one might be brought back for a look, even though Sue might not have been at all happy with her previous style of acting:

"How do you see these two approaches as different from the way you handled it originally?"

After the answer comes out, some prompting could be given to see what some of the benefits were in the original way of acting. After all, people normally act to gain something positive, even if it is only a short-term advantage. "What do you think was the advantage of the first way of handling it...even with all of its stated drawbacks?"

Examining the benefits of old behaviors is essential. The reason is that people must face up to the gain, no matter how small or perverse it is. If they do not recognize it, then they will be tempted to perform the same behavior again, not realizing what the temptation is. They will be caught off guard by the attraction to do what they did in the past, thinking they were past such "useless" behavior.

Goals in our intentional caring need to be realistic. They are meant to open up areas for consideration, to accept the person while pointing out apparently ineffective behavior and to refrain from imposing our own values on those with whom we are interacting.

In our conversation with a goal, one of our assumptions is that we are not doing psychotherapy, but instead, we are attempting to help people become self-critical; that is, critical in ways that enable them to evaluate complex factors in broad, interpersonal situations. Just as it is said, "Give a person a fish and feed them for a day; teach them to fish and feed them for a lifetime," intentional caring is designed to help people begin to examine their feelings and the styles of problem-solving that they use. In this way, they can become more attuned to how the problems they experience arise and how they might be prevented or dealt with more effectively.

Intentional Caring and Growth

Our purposeful conversation also assumes that people can grow. While this earth is not a perfect place to live, it is a place for optimum growth. Every crisis, every hardship, every argument, every emotion carries with it the potential for growth. Jesus assumed that the woman at the well was capable of and ready for growth. His conversation was designed to make available to the woman an opportunity for personal and spiritual growth.

Developmental psychologists like Erik Erikson[1] or Robert Kegan[2] point out that there are predictable stages of growth in human development. Christian educator James Fowler[3] suggests that there are also stages to spiritual development and that we are called to grow. Pastoral counselor Howard Clinebell[4] proposes a "holistic liberation-growth model" for pastoral care and counseling. Jungian psychologists like John Sanford[5] and Fritz Kunkel,[6] when looking at scripture, see the growth of the individual, or "individuation," as central to the gospel message. Scripture itself indicates that the Christian journey on earth is one of growing in holiness or sanctification (for example, Romans 6:19).

Intentional caring assumes that the present moment holds an opportunity for growth. Psychologist Rollo May points out that there is a close relationship between caring and intention. The root word in "intentional" is the word "to tend." "To tend" means "to take care of," but also has the meaning "to tend toward," or "to move toward" something.[7] Intentional caring moves us toward something in a process of growth and assumes that the present moment holds an opportunity for growth.

Our purposeful conversation makes available that opportunity for growth while not forcing growth to happen. For instance, a person who was distraught and depressed over a wayward daughter said,

"It seems like no matter which way I turn I am damned. If I make it hard on her and enforce all the rules, then I will be damned for her running away. If I let up on the rules and she goes out and gets pregnant, then I will be damned for making that happen, too."

"It sounds like you only know a God who damns you."

(Tears. Silence.) "I guess I have said that I believe in a God of love, but when it comes down to it, I live in fear of making mistakes and being punished for it."

"I wonder what it would be like for you if you approached this situation with your daughter believing in a God who loves and lets us learn from our mistakes."

In this situation the person is in the process of taking a major growth step in her spiritual relationship with God. This growth step has a major impact on her perception of how to conduct her life and how to raise her daughter. In turn, this growth will impact the daughter's ability to grow as well.

Growth implies that a person is not finished and, therefore, that he/she has a future. Many who come for care assume that they are trapped or that their future holds no promise. Someone may have lost a loved one and, in her grief, can see no future. An abused woman can see no way to escape from her marriage with the need to support a family and raise the children. Someone with a financial crisis cannot see how he will make it. A person with bad habits or addictive behavior does not know how it will ever be any different.

It is easy for us to be drawn into a belief that there is no way out. Yet in our conversation with a purpose we assume that growth is possible and that the future can be different. Jesus did not approach the woman at the well with the attitude that this woman was finished because of her poor choices (an attitude the disciples evidently had and which her community probably had). Jesus assumed that she had a future with a new purpose and way of living.

This is not to say that we have the answers or can see what the future holds. We can often only join the person in seeking revelation and believing that a way will open up that is not yet clearly seen. For instance, a woman living with a drug addicted spouse feels that it is destructive for her and for her children to stay in the marriage, but she has no idea how she could ever make it on her own and says,

"I cannot believe that it is good for the children to be around the drug habit. In fact, it is quite dangerous at times, to say nothing of the influence on them. I don't want them to grow up believing this is the way to live. I get nothing out of the relationship because he is always high and will not have a meaningful conversation with me. And he's spending all the money on drugs that we need to pay the bills."

"Sounds like you're up against the Red Sea, the Egyptians are approaching and there's no way out."

"Somehow God gave them a way out. Are you implying that there is a way out of this mess?"

"There is a story that says the Red Sea did not open until someone had the courage to stick their toe in the water and believe they could get through it somehow. Maybe we can look for ways for you to stick your toe in the water and see what happens."

There is no solution to the woman's problems at this point, but there is an assumption that there is a future and that some little acts of courage on her part may produce something different. What exactly that will be neither the caregiver nor the one seeking care knows.

To "stick her toe in the water" may mean to begin to think and behave differently right where she is. Perhaps she can go to some Al-Anon meetings and learn some different responses to her spouse. Possibly she could pray specifically for what she wants and ask for revelation. Maybe "sticking her toe in the water" would mean getting the facts of what it would take to move out, looking in the paper for apartments or a job. Or, "sticking her toe in the water" could mean using her active imagination to visualize what it would be like on her own, or visualizing coping with the things in life of which she is now afraid.[8] "Sticking her toe in the water" might mean coming to grips with the death of what she thought her future was going to be like with this husband and beginning to write for herself a new "future story" that has a different ending and perhaps different players.[9] As she grasps the possibility of a future and works toward it, she will grow.

Finally, growth often happens at moments when we say or do very little. It is somewhat ironical that our conversation with a goal actually takes us to those moments when words are hard to find or we are reduced to silence. Our assumption is that these are moments of real growth that we cannot control or make happen. What is most effective is our empathetic presence.

Chris Schlauch suggests that empathy is the essence of pastoral psychotherapy.[10] Empathy, he says, is a style of caring in which we try to find our way, or search our way, into the experience of another. Empathy allows us to gain access to the interior life of another person. At the same time, empathy creates an atmosphere and attitude toward life that is conveyed to the person needing care even when nothing is said.

To allow a person to speak what heretofore has been unspeakable in her life, to hear her pain or life story nonjudgmentally and to "walk in her shoes" as best we can provide an opportunity for deep growth to occur in the life of that individual. It is as if something is released and she is allowed to move forward. For instance, a person with unresolved grief finally comes to say,

> *"I've never said this before. I loved her and I've tried to pretend that everything was OK before she got sick. I've tried to remember her as almost a saint. But that's not the whole story. We had our fights. Even worse was when we didn't fight and she made me feel guilty or she played the martyr with one kind of illness or another. I hated those times. I even wished she would die so I could marry someone else. I can't believe I'm saying this. I really did love her."* (Tears. Silence.)
>
> *"I hear the pain of your whole reality—your love and your hate."* (Silence.)
>
> *"Do you think God can forgive me? I want to move on."*
>
> *"It sounds like you are open to forgiveness and are already moving on."*

Our conversation with a goal assumes that spiritual and emotional growth are possible even in the simplest of human exchanges where we empathetically care and, therefore, connect with another human being in a way that stimulates life. Sometimes very little is actually said.

Robert Kegan illustrates this with a story from his experience among the Hasidim. His story is about Rifka, who was questioning whether or not she could truly be a Hasid if she could buy something that was not kosher when she was in a hurry. She tells the experience of being in the Super Duper food store buying what she needed quickly. When in the store she passed a woman who had a child who was an "idiot" and for a moment Rifka saw her. That night Rifka could not go to sleep thinking of the woman and her child, and she cried.

"'…I cried for that mother vit her idiot vhat kept on living. I cried for that mother vhat had an idiot and vhass pricing the mustard. And I cried for the idiot vhat vhass life. He vhass life.'

'It's terrible,' I mumbled, not knowing what to say.

'Don't say this. Vhat is terrible?' she said. 'I'm telling you should know. I'm talking to you.

'That voman, that mother, ve did not say a vord to each other, but ve talked. Not till I came home vhass many hours later did I know ve talked. But ve talked. I heard her and she gave me. Vhat is terrible? You live, you talk. Ve talked. And you know vhat I thought vhen I vhass crying?

'I thought: I cry tonight now this mother vit her idiot vhat is so beautiful vhat is life, tomorrow she vill cry less.' "[11]

5. Intentional Caring: The Art of Questioning and Responding

Intentional caring utilizes conversation with a goal, which is more than ordinary conversation and is based upon assumptions we have about human nature, the purpose of life and our limited role as listeners. Yet, even when we are clear about our assumptions, we still must learn to question and respond in such a way that is congruent with our assumptions and does not unwittingly get in the way of either empathy or growth.

No matter what the situation, there comes a time when a question is appropriate. The problems inherent in developing and asking questions are numerous, though, and asking the right type of question is an artful pursuit. It is a skill that can be learned through understanding and the practice of a few basic principles.

Basic Principles

The first of these principles is to *ask as few questions as possible*. The reason for this is that anytime one breaks in to ask a question, it interrupts the flow of communication by the person seeking help. How many times have you been in the middle of explaining something and were interrupted over and over again by annoying questions? If the person had only waited a few moments, the answer would have been forthcoming. The person was just impatient or had to hear himself talk. (Caution: You are not actively listening if you are busy formulating questions.)

A second principle is to *make your questions short, clear and to the point.* Stress or high emotions produce situations in which diminished amounts of information can be received and understood. A poorly formed question will be harder for a distressed person to interpret than might normally be the case. Thus, a question must be clear and purposeful. Each question needs to be formulated and presented with the hope of eliciting specific data in a particular area.

Complex or compound sentences require a number of points to be addressed. This may cause confusion or result in part of the question going unanswered: "You say you haven't been feeling well and that your appetite isn't so good. How are you doing now?" (Does this question refer to the person's general health, appetite or both?) "Oh, I think I'm getting better now." (Is his general health improving, or is he referring to both his health and his appetite?)

Another element in good questioning is to *decide the type of question the situation calls for and act accordingly.* Questions can be divided into two types: *open* and *closed.* An open question is designed to get the person to deal with areas with a broad stroke. It is not a focused method of getting at specifics. It is a way of permitting the person seeking care to embark upon a topic without the encumbrances of too much pressure from the caregiver.

Here are some examples of open questions:

"Tell me a bit about how you've been feeling at work."

"What are your feelings when you have to call John and tell him you won't go out with him?"

"You say Mary upsets you. What do you mean?"

"Well, what are your plans for the future?"

Open questions are not designed to tie things together. On the contrary, they are meant to open previously packaged thoughts and feelings on an issue so they can be viewed together by you and the person you are helping. Since the goal is to encourage communication and freedom within the interpersonal interaction, most of our questions will be of this nature.

There are times, though, when closed questions are necessary. Usually closed questions are used when a detailed or a "yes" or "no" response is required. The time to use them normally occurs toward the end of the discussion on a topic when the caregiver is trying to tie things up in his or her mind.

> *"So how long did you date John?"*
> *"Are you afraid of confronting him, then?"*
> *"Where were you when this happened to you?"*

There is nothing wrong with using a closed question. A problem only occurs when it is used incorrectly, namely when the form is biased, and when the closed question is used inadvertently in place of an open one.

A biased question is a leading closed question. This is when the person is given only one of several choices for an answer. It is a style that forces the person to choose from a limited number of responses: "Anyone who could do something like that has to be callous, right?" (One choice.) "When she did that, did you think she was being cowardly or shy?" (Two choices.)

Such leading questions corner a person. Even if they are being guided toward a correct answer, the danger is always present that they are being forced to agree with your perception of the matter. Persons who can be quite suggestible may agree with you even if your perceptions are not correct. Others will feel like they are on a witness stand being led by lawyerlike questions that will block their experience of being heard empathetically.

A direct question does not have to be a leading one. In the first example above, the question could be phrased, "What do you think of someone who does something like that?" Or, if the person has made it evident that, in his opinion, the individual under discussion is in fact callous, you can phrase it accordingly: "From what you say, it sounds like you believe the person is callous."

Another important part of the art of questioning is *learning how to handle interruptions.* You already know to ask as few questions as possible so *you* do not interrupt the flow of information. But what if someone or something else demands momentary attention? If an unavoidable interruption occurs during your conversation, it needs to be handled carefully. If it isn't, the person may be turned off.

We have all been in situations where we were pouring out our hearts to someone and have been interrupted by a telephone call or a visitor coming in to see the person we were addressing. If a caregiver excused himself and came back saying, "Let's see, now where were we?" the one receiving care might be thinking, "Well, if you don't remember, I guess we were nowhere!"

When we are interrupted from the outside, we should try to minimize the negative effect of the temporary distraction. This can be done by trying to remember the last few words said when the telephone rings or when someone interrupts. Then when we have finished quickly with whomever has intruded, we can return and say, "Let's see, you were saying…" (noting the last several words the person had said). This demonstrates your interest in the person and gets the conversation back on target.

Focusing Your Questions

Your questions will be most helpful if they are infrequent, simple, purposeful and open (unless a closed question is necessary). Furthermore, each *series* of questions should be designed to uncover not isolated facts and feelings, but a web of related factors, thoughts and feelings that comprise a description of the problem itself and of the person's perception of it. For example, if a youth is telling us about problems finding employment, questions regarding how he is searching for a new position, what educational background he has, what types of positions he's held in the past and what his hopes and expectations for his future are should provide us with a better description of his situation.

Feelings and perceptions about a problem can be explored on at least three levels: personal, interpersonal and environmental. In seeking information, we are, in fact, looking simultaneously at all three of these areas.

The strictly *personal* level is an unobservably unique one. Our personality is responsible for the unique way we view ourselves and the world. No matter how much someone loves us, no matter how close someone is to us, no one views us exactly as we view ourselves. And, because of our special makeup and environmental history, no one views the world exactly as we do. There will be many who occasionally see us as we see ourselves. Likewise, some will agree with one of our opinions of the world, but our total personal view of ourselves and the world is unique.

Therefore, one of the areas that interests us when a person comes to us for help is the strictly personal one of how he or she feels and thinks about the current situation. The same kind of predicament can be viewed and reacted to in any number of ways. Our job is to ferret out this person's particular view and help make it clearer to him or her.

For instance, if your friend's twenty-year-old daughter has decided to move into an apartment in the heart of the city, there can be a number of ways this action can be seen by a mother. One of them is, "She's too young! I won't let her do it."

This mother is critical in a negative way. Her feeling is that she must act in a domineering manner to protect her daughter. No thought is given to the positive possibilities of the move, or the potential failure of such an action. To open up this area so the person can look at it more fully, a number of questions might have to be asked, such as:

"Have you discussed with your daughter when you think she will be old enough to move out?"

"What do you think will happen when you put your foot down and tell her she can't leave?"

"It sounds like you're pretty upset about this. How do you feel about this whole matter?"

"What's been going on that led up to her making the decision at this time?"

In the questions above, the goal is to get the woman to look at her own feelings and thoughts, and at her resultant plans regarding the situation. It is also designed to let her see how her style of viewing and dealing with the world is having an impact on her daughter.

Another mother might view the same situation in a slightly different way: "Mary is going to move out. I must admit I don't like it....I guess I'm worried about her, but she has to make the move sooner or later."

This woman seems more in touch with her *own* feelings regarding her daughter's decision. She also seems less critical in a negative way. In addition, she appears to be more aware of her role and her daughter's rights. Yet, there are still a number of questions that could be asked to help the woman look at her feelings and thoughts more directly:

> *"What kinds of things are you worried about?"*
> *"When would you have preferred she make the move?"*
> *"What did she say when she told you about the move?"*
> *"You seem ambivalent about her decision. How do you feel about it?"*

Naturally, the above only illustrate several types of questions that could be asked. The idea is to get the person to focus in on herself. In doing this, we try to put her feelings, no matter what they are, on the table. The more she can see her fears, concerns, joys and frustrations, the better it is for all concerned.

Also, we can and should try to support the person without supporting her actions. For example, if she says, "I know I sound silly being so upset, but I can't help it," a reply can be, "Why is it silly?" The person may say, "Well, she has to move out sometime." At that point the response can be, "That may be true, and I think you recognize the fact, but it's still OK to worry. You can't deny the way you feel."

Focusing on the overlapping *interpersonal* area is as important as uncovering someone's inner, personal feelings. In exploring the interpersonal area, the questions posed should be directed to the style of interaction that someone uses with one or more people involved in the problem being presented.

Take the following situation, for example:

> *"My boss said I wasn't producing enough, that I was wasting time. I asked him whether he wanted quality work or a lot of garbage. And when I told my coworker what he said, do you know what she suggested? She actually said I spend too much time on the phone. Can you believe that? I told her she was missing the point."*

This worker is obviously denying there is a problem. Instead of hearing the complaint, she is blocking the information from getting through and is taking a very defensive position. Getting through to this woman is going to be quite difficult, but a number of questions and comments may help open up the area a bit:

> *"What prompted your boss to talk to you about this?"*
> *"When he started telling you what he thought, how did you feel?"*
> *"How did he react when you told him what you thought?"*
> *"What is of positive value in what your coworker or boss said?"*

The idea is to chip away at what is going on, not to mount a frontal attack. Once again, falling into the savior complex must be avoided at all cost. The goal is not to force the person to see the light, but rather to help shine at least a thin ray of light on the situation. By trying too hard to force the person to see a particular point or by being even the slightest bit overly direct with this type of person, a rebuff may result.

Finding out about a person's *environment* is also an important goal. Just as the person's inner feelings and interpersonal interactions have an impact on the outcome of a situation, environmental pressures and resources can also significantly affect the results.

Social environment is comprised of a number of factors. The family group, vocational opportunities and issues, neighborhood resources and liabilities, social networks (such as religious affiliations or clubs) and other outside sources of support or frustration all contribute to how a person deals with life's challenges.

In the case of the daughter leaving home to get an apartment for herself, the social environment could be explored in terms of both the mother and the daughter. As the mother speaks about both her misgivings and positive feelings about the move, a number of questions might naturally come up that could help uncover relevant patterns in the environment. With regard to the daughter, the following questions might be asked:

"What kind of neighborhood is she moving to?"

"Will she be living with a friend? Does she have friends close by?"

"What does she perceive as the advantages and disadvantages of having her own apartment?"

"Will it be easier for her to get to her job and the educational and social environments she is interested in?"

With the mother in mind, other questions might arise:

"How will your life change when your daughter moves?"

"How will the move affect other people in the family? What do they think about her getting her own place?"

The Level of the Question

Questions must be worded in a way that the person can easily understand. We might be tempted to use theological or psychological jargon as we begin to learn how to question. The following story illustrates the point:

A novice plumber's assistant wrote to the National Bureau of Standards to ask if he could use hydrochloric acid to clean out drainage pipes. In response, he received the following message from one of the workers: "The efficacy of hydrochloric acid is indisputable, but the corrosive residue is incompatible with metallic permanence." Upon getting this letter, the plumber's helper sent the following note to the worker at the Bureau: "I really appreciate your help. Thank you for letting me know it's OK to use it."

The worker showed this reply to a colleague. His coworker reacted by saying, "You always get carried away with the jargon; now we have to send him another note, but this time I'll write it." The letter he sent him was as follows: "We cannot assume responsibility for the production of toxic and noxious residue from hydrochloric acid and I suggest you use an alternative procedure."

This letter also secured a response from the plumber's assistant. It said something to the effect of, "Yes, I know hydrochloric acid works all right. Someone else has already written to tell me about it."

Finally, the director of the National Bureau of Standards

heard about the incident and decided to send the plumber's helper a final, brief, to-the-point note.

"Don't use hydrochloric acid. It eats the hell out of pipes."

To get our point across and to avoid being misunderstood, we must try to be clear and direct in what we say. Otherwise we run the risk of having an additional, unwarranted communication problem to contend with in our interaction.

In addition to using clear and direct language that keeps the question on the level of the person seeking care, we must also ask questions on an emotional level that the person can presently understand. In John 14:12 Jesus says to the disciples, "I have many things to say to you, but you cannot bear them now." The disciples were not ready to hear or to struggle with greater revelation at that time. Out of respect for the disciples, Jesus refrains from sharing everything he knows.

The same is true in our intentional caring. The level of our questioning needs to be directed to what the person can bear or understand at the present time. We may ask questions that cause a person to think a little more deeply about a situation, but our question cannot be way ahead of where they are. We may have accurate insight into the nature of their problem, but they cannot bear to hear it or to think about it at the moment.

For instance, in the case of unresolved grief shared in the last chapter, we might have suspected early on that the man was blocked in his ability to look realistically at how things were before his wife died. But early on in our conversation he would not be able to bear the thought that he not only loved her, but hated her at times. The level of our questions needs to be close to where he is. Early in our conversation it would be inappropriate to ask, "I hear you saying only how great things were with your wife, but I'm wondering if you ever had a fight or if there were things you didn't like?" Because the question is too far ahead of where he is, it would probably produce a response that denied the reality of his unspoken anger at her. But keeping our hunches in mind we might ask, "Can you tell me more about what it was like to live with your wife, especially when she was so sick?" The level of this question is closer to what he can bear to hear.

Getting the Complaint in Detail

Very often in our intentional caring, the complaint or problem that the person brings to us is skipped over too lightly. When the complaint has not been voiced in detail, we can get bogged down in trying to give general advice or useless supportive statements and jump to find quick, easy solutions. This can only lead to frustration for the helper and possibly annoyance or feelings of futility on the part of the troubled individual who came for help.

Consequently, getting specific details is given first priority when a problem is reported. *What, when, with whom* and *under what circumstances* are questions that need to be answered. Without answers to them, proceeding further may be a rocky, precarious adventure.

When a fellow says he is in trouble because he feels inadequate we need to find out:

What does he mean by "inadequate"? Everyone uses words in a slightly different manner, so find out in detail what this person means by "inadequate" in reference to himself.

When does he feel inadequate? Do not accept "all the time" as an answer. If he says this, then ask him when does he feel more inadequate than usual.

With whom does he feel inadequate? And, for that matter, with whom does he feel less inadequate? How does he account for the difference?

Under what circumstances does he feel inadequate? In other words, where is he and what kinds of things is he thinking and feeling during, before and after the experience?

By getting the details, the caregiver and the troubled person can look at the issue in a problem-solving manner. This process is in itself curative. By looking at the facts, a feeling starts to emerge that "Gee, there are reasons and factors behind my feelings and behavior. Maybe I can do something about it other than sit around and worry."

Here is a brief illustration of how the reported problem of inadequacy might be dealt with:

"I don't know, Jill. Lately I just feel so behind everyone, so inadequate."

"Arlene, I don't quite know what you mean when you say 'inadequate.' "

"You know, inadequate, inadequate...I don't know how else to put it."

"I guess what I'm getting at is that people experience things in different ways. When I get down, for example, I feel sort of empty. Other people say when they get blue, they feel off in a corner. How would you describe it when you feel inadequate?"

"Oh. Well, I think I see what you mean, but I still don't think I can tell you...."

"Just do your best."

"Well, I guess I feel sort of, well, like less. Yes, that's it. I feel less."

"Less?"

"Yeah, like smaller, like a little child who is awkward, stupid and well...almost like my head is full of cotton because I can't seem to function smoothly."

"Can you give me an example of when you felt like that?"

"Oh, I can give you plenty of examples. I feel that way all the time now."

"Just give me an illustration that comes to mind."

"You know it's funny, I can't think of any now...(long silence). I just can't think of any."

"Well, how about an incident that really brought the point home. One that made you say, 'Good grief! I really feel inadequate. I really feel like a small little child.' " (Note reuse of Arlene's own words.)

"That's easy! At work just this morning I felt that way when one of the salesmen came in and asked me for information on one of the new drugs the company is marketing. I got so nervous I fell apart. I couldn't find the file, much less the handout he needed. Finally, my boss come in and found it immediately. I felt like such a jerk."

"Do you feel that way only with the sales personnel?"

"No. That's just it. I also feel it with the product managers and the advertising execs as well."

"How about your immediate boss?"

"No, not really. Sometimes, I guess."

"When?"

"Well, once when she asked me to take her place while she was temporarily taking over her boss's job at a convention in Boston. I thought I was going to pieces. The thing that surprised me is that I always thought I could do her job. It's not that hard, you know."

"Did you have ample time to prepare for the position?"

"No, that's just it. She burst in one day and said, 'Tomorrow we have to go to Boston and John (her boss) can't make it, so I'll have to fill in for him and you'll have to take over for me.' I was flabbergasted."

"If you had more time, do you think you could have done it?"

"Not well."

"Better than you did?"

"Well, I guess so. Yes."

"How about if the sales rep had called before coming over and said he would be picking up the info on the new drug in a half hour; do you think you could have found it?"

"Oh, sure. But that's silly. I shouldn't have gotten so upset just because he came in without warning."

"Well, maybe you're right. But the issue is you don't always feel and function inadequately."

"So, big deal."

"It is a big deal. The more you can find out about when and how you start to feel inadequate, the more you can see what's causing it and how to handle it. At the very least now, you can see that when you're caught off guard or surprised, you get a little startled and shaken."

"But why should that happen?"

"Well, there could be many reasons. What are you worried will happen when someone drops an assignment on you...(etc.)?"

The idea is to get people to look at what's happening, what they are feeling, who is with them and other similar details. Get them away from amorphous floating feelings of helplessness. Good questions not only elicit details that are helpful for the caregiver, but also bring to light data that the person seeking help may not have examined previously. The process of gathering information is in itself a helpful process.

Answering Questions with Questions

To jump in prematurely and offer feedback without giving time for both of you to grasp the specifics of the problem is sheer folly. Watch what happens when the bait is taken by the caregiver to give advice too early in the game:

Mr. J. has been speaking for several minutes about his marital problems. During this time he has highlighted the fact that he is often busy at work, and that this irritates his wife. Suddenly he stops and asks, "What do you think I can do to make the marriage work better?"

In response the caregiver quickly says, "Possibly you could spend more time with your wife. What do you think?"

"That's what everyone says. I wish it were that simple. What am I supposed to do? Give up my business? So, we'll be together and have no money, then what? You're just like everyone else. You see only one side of it."

Another example that illustrates how easy it is to go astray when responding with a comment instead of a question is as follows:

Ms. B. had been speaking in a derogatory manner about her sister for about ten minutes. She then said, "And added to all I've told you, she also just grabs my clothes and wears them without asking me. Isn't she a bitch?"

Feeling the pressure of the question, the caregiver responded almost without thinking, "It's true it seems that she isn't taking your feelings into consideration, but...."

Quickly Ms. B. interjected, having heard almost exactly what she wanted to hear, "I knew you'd feel that way. I'm glad you do. I was pretty sure I should move out and leave her holding the lease, but now I'm positive!"

The problem in the above two interactions is similar. The listeners failed to question the question and return to a silent stance. They failed to return the focus to the person in distress.

Perhaps the caregivers were concerned that they would be "rigid and cowardly" merely to reflect the question back to the one seeking help. Jokes are often made in therapeutic circles about "super nondirective therapists" who answer everyone's

question with a reflection of that question, like the experience of
a worker at a clinic who needed directions on the first day there:

> *"Excuse me, doctor, can you tell me where the men's room is?"*
> *"You say you want to know where the men's room is?"*
> *"Yes, I'd like to know where it is."*
> *"It sounds like you'd really like to know."*
> *(In an annoyed voice), "Yes, I would like to know."*
> *"It seems like you're annoyed that you don't know where the*
> *men's room is."*
> *(Now in an angry voice), "Yes, I want to know where it is; are you*
> *going to tell me or not?"*
> *"It seems you're angry at me because you don't know where the*
> *men's room is."*
> *(Moving around the desk toward the therapist) "What, me*
> *angry? Don't be silly. When I rip up your office now it's going to be an*
> *act of love!"*

While it is true that one can be too nondirective and ask
questions at inappropriate times, in reality, these occasions are
rare. A low-key, well-directed question will be appropriate far
more often than not.

Often we feel that when someone asks a question, *not* to
answer it is an evasion. However, this misses the principle
behind querying questions that are put to us. The reason a question is answered with a question is to *make sure that we fully
understand the question asked by the one seeking care.* In addition, it
indicates to the person seeking care that he or she is responsible
for working toward a personal solution.

Answering questions without exploring them before-
hand does two things. First, it supports infantile reactions in
those seeking help by implicitly agreeing that they cannot
come up with answers themselves. Secondly, it stops the communication without allowing the person to reflect on the question to see what it may mean from a number of angles. This
latter point is very important because the actual question may
be very different from the way it looks on first blush. For
instance:

"Are there many people like me who are depressed? (This question seems to be one that requires a "yes" or "no" answer on the basis of the caregiver's knowledge of the world's statistics on depression.)

"I'm not sure what you're asking."

"Well, I just want to know if there are more people like me."

"What prompts the question?"

"Well, I guess I've been thinking, I wonder if I'm normal, or if I'm a useless freak?"

"Can you tell me a little more about these feelings you've been having about yourself?"

(Person begins relating fears of going crazy, thoughts about being alone and feelings of hopelessness.)

In the above illustration, the caregiver would never have gotten to the subsequent material if the first question had been answered without being explored. Also, to answer what had seemed initially to be the question would have been to move in the wrong direction.

Sometimes it is not easy to answer a question with a question because the one seeking help may resent it at first. However, having a questioning attitude is essential because it demonstrates that you're not the "magic answer machine," and it shows faith in the person's ability to solve his or her own problem with a little support. The following example illustrates this point:

"What do you think I should do?"

"Well, what have you come up with?"

"Nothing; that's why I'm asking you."

"I hear your question, but I'm sure you've given this problem some thought, and I'd like to hear what you've come up with—whatever it might be."

"Is this all I can expect? More questions?"

"What were your expectations?"

"That you would give me some answers. I could ask myself questions without you."

"Yes, you could, but there is some value if we both look at the questions you've been asking yourself. Sometimes speaking about them out loud is helpful. So let's look at what you've been thinking and feeling

about the situation. Now what kinds of things have you been feeling about the problem you've just related?"

Dealing with Unsatisfactory Responses

There are times when a question is asked but the answer received is insufficient in some fashion. Possibly it is incomplete, vague or does not seem even to be directed at what was asked. When this occurs it is sometimes helpful to take steps to clear up the situation so a better answer can be secured.

The first step is to mentally review how the question was phrased. Possibly it was a poor or inadequately developed question. The next step is to attempt to rephrase it and present it again. If this still does not seem to produce results, we have to make a judgment: Is the person so sensitive to this topic that it is difficult for him or her to answer it? Should I drop further questioning for now? Or should I press further, noting that the person seems to be having difficulty understanding or answering what is being asked?

Such a judgment is difficult to make. If the person seems hypersensitive, then possibly it would be best to bring the issue up later on, or even at another meeting. However, in most cases, pressing on gently would at least bring this area a bit more out in the open. To do this, a simple statement such as, "I guess I'm not making myself clear because I still don't know where you stand (or how you feel about)..." should bring the person sufficiently out in the open on the issue.

Transitions Between Topics

Sometimes a confused or ambiguous response to a question stems from the fact that the caregiver has jumped from topic to topic without giving enough thought to making any connection between the different areas. While a relationship may exist in the mind of the caregiver, the person seeking assistance might not be in a position to see the connection and feel jolted by the change in focus.

Our awkwardness in changing topics may cause anxiety in

the other person. A transitional technique is sometimes helpful in preventing such anxiety. This is especially so during the middle or near the end of the conversation.

In the beginning of the contact, we should try not to interrupt the person unless it is essential to do so. In most cases, opening up and venting one's emotions are more important initially than organization or expansion of the information. Consequently, when the contact first begins, listening attentively is the most valuable "action" we can take.

After fifteen minutes to a half an hour has passed, though, enough clues should be out in the open for both people present to examine together. At this point, and *at the pace of the one seeking care*, the caregiver can start to focus and expand on a number of areas.

Most of us do not have unlimited time to spend with a friend, employee or family member, so wanting to cover a number of perspectives in working out a problem is quite natural. To do this efficiently and smoothly, knowing how to make a definite transition can be helpful.

When enough material has been presented by the person to permit a clear understanding of the issues at hand, the following steps should be taken to move the process along: (1) interrupt, (2) clarify material gathered through feedback, and (3) change the topic to an allied area.

Let's say a friend of yours, Bill, is reporting how disgusted he is working as a truck driver. The point has come in the narrative where you think you have a good sense of the situation in which he finds himself. The question that seems to follow logically is, "What else can he do other than stay in what he terms a 'dead-end position'?" How do you move on to this area without offending Bill who still seems deep in the story, but whom you must stop soon because you have an appointment in twenty minutes?

Here is how the three steps can be put into action: "Excuse me a minute Bill. Let me see if I have it straight. You say being a driver has turned out to be a dead-end position. The only way you can make more money is to work longer hours, and you're already putting in fifty-two hours a week. What's making it even more frustrating is that you feel the work is getting too heavy for you and you're tired of getting stuck with any old truck—often without a heater and sometimes with questionable brakes. Well, since all this stuff is getting to you, what do you think are the options open to you, other than continuing as a driver?"

When moving from topic to topic, it is important to give a good summary of what you've heard before moving on to another area. Sometimes you may not have gotten the exact impression the person is trying to convey. Thus, giving summarized feedback allows the narrator a chance to correct any misconceptions.

In the above illustration, Bill might have stepped in and said something to alter the impression you had. For instance, "Everything you said is on the mark, but believe me, it's not the heavy work that bothers me so much. It's just that there seems to be no future if I stay where I am."

Once this correction takes place, the caregiver takes note of it and moves on to the next area. "Well, OK. Given the fact there's no future, Bill, what's open to you in terms of options to change the situation?"

Special Guidelines for Responding

In our intentional caring we will not always respond with a question. There are other ways of responding and interacting that we will do well to learn and understand if we are to facilitate a "conversation with a goal."

Pacing. Each person is unique. How readily someone can assimilate information and confront personal patterns of dealing with the world is quite variable. Furthermore, each person's readiness to deal with these kinds of issues varies from time to time. At times we are ready and anxious to move ahead. At other times we do not want to face reality. People try to confront us with the truth and we do not want to hear it.

As caregivers, we should keep this variability in mind and pace our conversation at a rate comfortable for the person with whom we are dealing. Going too fast can be just as unproductive as going too slow.

A number of things can tip us off when we are moving along at too *fast* a pace. The person may be confused about what we are saying. We may be saying things that the person is having great difficulty accepting. Or the person may quite emotionally demonstrate anger, respond with quick compliance to our interpretation or become very anxious.

Moving along too quickly can be caused by several factors. In some cases, it might be the caregiver's lack of patience with the progress being made and a feeling of futility about the changes occurring. Pacing problems due to impatience and frustration can be handled to a great extent by recognizing the presence of these feelings and not permitting them to govern the course of the interaction. Another step that may help is to remind ourselves regularly of the value of active listening and support of the person, and the lack of wisdom in a hurried intervention on our part.

Another common reason we sometimes behave precipitously is to demonstrate personal expertise. This exhibitionism may show itself in a number of ways. One example of it is when we try to show how well we can interpret what is going on. This attempt to display a special talent for putting things together is immature and does not help develop the resources of the person who seeks our help.

Going too *slowly* can also be a problem. A person may be anxious to look at personal patterns and styles, and we may hold back. When we hold back, it indicates to the person that we are fearful of proceeding; that, in fact, there is something to be afraid of, embarrassed about or concerned with. When this occurs, we need to take a careful look at our view of the person and the type of material under discussion. Possibly we are underestimating the one with whom we are working. Another reason could be that we do not really want progress to occur. Let's face it; most of us occasionally like to be in control and tend to be authoritarian with certain types of people. If they are marching ahead without our "precious guidance," they may falter. In fact, the fear is they may realize we are not such great know-it-alls and they do not need us as much as they thought. One of the aims of our conversation with a goal is that the other person remain as independent as possible.

But at an unconscious level, this may not be what we want. That is why we have to keep a close check on ourselves as caregivers.

Problems with pacing in general are due to a lack of appreciation of the resiliency of people and a lack of awareness of what makes people upset—that is, of their sensitive zones. Wondering whether you are moving along fast enough is not really a problem. The very people we are working with help us determine the proper pace. They give us continual feedback as to whether we are moving along at the wrong pace.

When we get the message that we are rushing along or holding up the bandwagon, we should take the opportunity to reflect on why this is occurring and on the feelings we have that prompt such errors. By doing this we can cut down on the number of times we do it.

If, for instance, we see that we are always putting on the "savior" mantle with one type of individual, then we can learn to correct it and recognize how this kind of person elicits this behavior from us. One of the exciting things about caregiving is that the more we try to work carefully with others who are in distress, the more we learn about ourselves. By being sensitive to ourselves as well as to those who need care, we cannot help but improve our self-examination skills and interpersonal communication talents.

Dealing with specifics. When someone has a problem, frequently friends and family will avoid the issue by responding with very general supportive phrases such as, "Don't worry, everything will be all right," and "You'll see, everything will turn out for the best." When these responses are questioned by the person, they are often followed by more of the same: "How do you know things will work out?" "Oh, they just will. You'll see."

Phrases like these reflect the need of some people to avoid dealing with an anxiety-producing topic by clamping a sweet lid on the subject as quickly as possible. Such generalizations can also be hazardous to the person's health. Too much support and reassurance can actually be detrimental because they discourage self-examination, and stifle the pursuit of real solutions to real problems. Furthermore, if we start pouring on the syrupy support, the person may start to wonder why we protest so much.

They may start to think that perhaps the problem is far more serious than they had ever thought.

Meeting vague negative feelings with amorphous positive ones is of little value to the person we are dealing with and should, therefore, be avoided. The hope that we as caregivers offer for the future is based in reality, not on sweet dreams. Real hope is tied to knowing the specifics of the situation. When someone tells us that they are anxious today and do not know why, we do not just tell them to forget it. We ask them to tell us about their day. We imply that if they are anxious, there must be a cause.

In response, we sometimes hear, "Nothing unusual happened. I just don't know what it's all about." This response means nothing. Continued pursuit is in order. "Well, let's go over what happened and how you felt about things today anyway. Your anxiety has to be caused by something."

One of the important features about the above response is the inclusion of the word *felt*. It may be that nothing happened in the outside world to upset the anxious person. However, something might have keyed off a thought or feeling about a sensitive area in the person's life. That is why knowing when people started feeling the way they do and what they were thinking and doing prior to the feeling's onset is important material to elicit.

Pointing out behaviors. As part of our effort to point out specifics, we should try to focus on behavioral patterns that can provide essential information. For example, by demonstrating *comparisons* and *contradictions* in what is said, felt and done, people are able to see where some of their confusion in getting hold of a troublesome issue really lies.

If people report they do not work too hard, but their schedule says they put in sixty hours per week, we have to wonder about the contradiction. If a woman is nice to one sister and nasty to the other, we have to question it. If a male truck driver says no one likes him because he is not college educated, and he has at least three female friends who call him and see him as an interesting man, this whole area of self-image has to be investigated.

By comparing messages and behaviors, or reflecting contradictory ones, we open up the possibility for the other person to reflect on the connections and contradictions too. The person may then be able to view things in a different light and alter how he or she feels about or deals with an issue.

Questioning generalizations. Dr. Albert Ellis has long been a leader in behavioral psychology. One of his approaches to dealing with people is to uncover and replace the illogical thinking patterns they have. Dr. Aaron Beck has done similar work with depressed patients.[1]

Too often our thoughts get us into trouble. They express beliefs that are myths, false generalizations and broad sweeping statements and bear little resemblance to reality. In other words, broad statements like the following would have to be questioned:

> *"I should be able to be nice to people (i.e., everyone)."*
> *"There's no reason why people (i.e., everyone) shouldn't like me."*
> *"He's my father and he means well, so I shouldn't get angry at him."*

Generalizations and superlatives like these need to be examined carefully. Too often people say things that are not criticized by others because they seem to be only exaggerating. This may be so, but when such exaggerations are left unchallenged, even though the person saying them does not *really* believe what he is saying, they can still have an adverse effect.

In the first statement above, the question should be asked, "Why should you be able to be nice to everyone?" In the next instance, "What makes you think that everyone should like you?"

In the final example, the questioning should be directed at what occurred between the person and her father. This could then be followed by exploring the possibility of the feeling being a natural one, even though it might be one that she regrets having expressed.

> *"How did you happen to get angry at your father?"*
> *"Well, he just kept telling me how skinny I was getting and that I should eat more. He felt I was neglecting myself, just to look like a model. He kept harping and harping on it until I blew up. Like I said, I*

really shouldn't have gotten angry. He only had my best interests at heart."

"I'm confused. You didn't get angry at him because he had your best interests at heart, did you?"

"No. I got angry because of his harping."

"So, I'm not clear why you're not expected to get angry when someone harps on something, even if he is your father."

"Well, I guess it's to be expected, but I would rather have controlled myself."

"You might rather have controlled yourself, but would you agree that it's not so surprising that you got angry, given the circumstances?"

"Yes, I can see that now. I guess it was sort of natural."

Many times people operate on premises that are based on philosophical extremes. Many of the philosophies are ones that are too ideal to be attained completely. They are designed to provide goals and direction, not to be taken literally.

When someone says, "I shouldn't be so lazy," or some other such general statement, they have to be questioned. A helpful response to a hasty generalization like the one above is, "Where is it written that you should never be lazy?"

In this case, we are not trying to compromise another's philosophy of life. Rather, we are trying to point to reality. We are trying to recognize that while a person can seek to reach an ideal, he should not castigate himself *as if* everyone else has attained it already and he, the weak one, has not. Such a reaction will only lead to despondency and despair, rather than a clear recognition of the factors involved in why he did not get as far as he originally desired.

Giving feedback. In helping others put their behavior in perspective and put absurd thinking to rest, we give feedback, not advice. Advice is direction...from *above*. Feedback is reflection from an equal who is trying to consider the issues from a different vantage point.

As caregivers, we usually provide little new knowledge. Rather, we are involved primarily in questioning the issues from various angles so that the person can make a decision regarding future action. Given another opportunity to talk with the person, we could problem-solve and imagine how similar situations could be handled in a different fashion in the future. Persons who need care act on their own. Our goal is not to take over their decision-making powers through the provision of "gems of wisdom." Rather, we act more as a consultant, a nondirective catalyst.

In giving feedback, we are also supporting and modeling a problem-solving, open-ended approach to life's problems. We are encouraging people to be their own detectives. Self-examination and the determination of the specific circumstances of a situation are encouraged. When we ask, "When did it happen? Whom were you with at the time? How did you feel at the time? How did you feel just before and after the event? et cetera," we are priming them to ask themselves these same questions in the future.

Showing acceptance. By being empathetic and maintaining a fact-finding approach, we give people the message that we can accept them at the same time that we question their behavior. Initially, when questioned or asked to give an illustration of what they mean, people may take it as an intrusion, or they may be confused or feel threatened.

"Do you think I did wrong by the way I handled it?"
"What makes you say that?"
"Well, by the fact that you're questioning me on it."
"No. I just thought we'd get a better look at what went on so we could have a better chance to see why it turned out the way it did. By questioning, we might be able to get a broader view of things."

Eventually, when people deal with you enough, they begin to anticipate the questioning. They will say something and then go on to say, "I know. You're going to want an illustration of what I'm talking about." As people begin to see the questioning as a way to open up the issues for examination, rather than as a means to demonstrate wrongdoing on their part, they will provide information more readily.

As we know, the more comfortable we feel with someone, the more likely we are to venture out into new and sensitive areas of discussion. Likewise, when we feel the person accepts us and is interested not in harping on our failings but in working with us to improve our coping talents, we are more apt to challenge our old assumptions and make changes in the way we view and act upon things.

Evaluating first, changing second. Patience and reflection are encouraged in caregiving as a first step toward untangling whatever problem the person is facing. Often, when a call for help is made, there is an implicit belief on the part of the person that *radical* change is needed: "I just can't go on this way. I've got to do something or I'm going to go crazy."

To accept this premise, though, would be a hasty mistake. Radical change—or any major change for that matter—may not, in fact, be needed. A reasonable response to a statement of this sort is to encourage looking at the situation first to see what is actually happening: "Well, let's look at what's going on first. What's happened that made you feel this way?"

By responding in this way, you are putting the emphasis on examining the situation rather than putting the person on notice that the objective of the two of you working together is to change him or her.

While a person may exclaim, "I've got to change!" and may indeed eventually do so, there is usually a resistance to change as well. People naturally fear change. We all think to a certain degree, "Better the devil we know than the one we don't."

In encouraging people to look at and evaluate the factors involved, we are not trying to fool them until their guard is down so we can zap them with the truth, or so they can mend their ways and sweep out the old and bring in the (our) new ways. In fact, in many situations simply a slightly different perspective on the situation is all that is needed to make a real difference in how the situation is handled. Wisdom, which is the accumulation and mature application of knowledge, recognizes the potency of a minor, but *true,* shift in our train and style of thinking.

Vows of totally changing one's ways by people under stress are promises made in the wind. They may have impact when they come up in a novel. We may feel confident that Dickens' grumpy, miserly Scrooge meant business when he said, "I shall keep Christmas every day of the year." In real life, and especially in the caring environ, big change is not sought after simply because it may not be needed, or for that matter, be possible.

Being patient. In the cases where some change is required, it will not be accomplished overnight. Assimilation of new material and trial-and-error learning take time.

Think of how long it takes us to change our minds. Even in a discussion with other "flexible, open-minded people," amending an opinion of our own can be a big deal. We can be stating our arguments and hearing better ones presented by someone else, but we will still hold on to our viewpoint...at least temporarily, for we do not want them to know they are right and we (heaven forbid!) are wrong.

The same is true with those we try to help. There is an understandable resistance to accepting new pieces of information that do not fit established habits of thinking. Also, since learning is a gradual process, we cannot expect people to change behavior quickly and effectively.

The process of reflection, practice, questioning, thinking about new behavior and risking a new style of action takes time. Old behavior was not born overnight, and it will not be replaced in a short span of time.

In following these simple techniques in questioning and responding, the problems people bring to us will not seem so overwhelming to them nor to us. It is important not to expect too much. Ironically, the real "miracles" occur when we do not "expect a miracle" (which often means trying to manufacture a miracle). The "miracles" that do occur are small surprises that follow from using commonsense techniques and accomplishing something positive by giving people in distress the message that someone will listen to them and work as an equal with them in their need. If there is any "miracle," it is the miracle of the caring process in which we focus on our simple, caring questioning and responding, and wait to be surprised by God.

6. Stages of a
Caring Exchange

When we are actively caring for someone, we must observe and keep track of many things in the course of our intentional conversation. A simple organizational guideline can help us keep perspective and know where to go next. Such a guideline will help us direct the conversation productively.

While our intentional conversations are uniquely creative with every new caring exchange, there are still predictable stages that usually occur in the conversation, whether that conversation happens for an hour over lunch with a friend or takes place in a more formal meeting set up to talk about a problem. Remembering the stages will help us keep our focus in the conversation. We can remember the stages by remembering the word **CREATE**. The letters of this word remind us of the stages of the caring exchange: (1) *C*ontact, (2) *R*evelation, (3) *E*laboration, (4) *A*lternatives, (5) *T*ying it up, (6) *E*valuation.

Contact

The first stage of a caring exchange involves the initial contact that we have with a person. Our initial contact with a person and the problem being experienced can occur in a variety of ways. The person may call on the phone or be present in a room with us when the topic is introduced. The topic may be brought up immediately or after a good deal of time has been spent passing pleasantries.

In some cases, the problem may not be brought out in the open until we notice something and give the person an opening.

In our everyday contact with people, we will want to be alert to clues given to us so that we do not miss the opportunity for a caring conversation. We will want to be alert and not afraid to follow up on hints that come from a subtle change of voice or facial expression or a curious way that a person is telling a story. (A review of chapter 2 will remind us of our resistances that affect this initial stage of contact.)

For example, we may get nonverbal signs that prompt us to say something like, "What's the matter, John? You seem sad all of a sudden." Or the person may say something that tips us off to the fact that he wants to discuss something. "From what you're saying, you seem to be really concerned over your son's school problems." In many instances, however, the topic is brought up directly and a clear statement is made such as "I want to talk to you about something."

No matter how the plea is made, the type of initial response we make can have a great impact on the ultimate effectiveness of the caring exchange. If we express shock, try to avoid the issue or assume a formal "interviewer's voice," we run the risk of shutting off the interaction. The nature of our initial contact with a person, then, determines if any of the other stages of our caring exchange will occur at all.

How we react should be governed by the way *we* would like to be treated in a similar situation. Certainly, we would appreciate it if the response included a natural expression of interest in hearing about the difficulty by someone who is not anxious about what we will say. Then, following the expression of interest and concern, we would probably appreciate some silent space to permit us to reveal our general perception of our problem.

Revelation

Things have probably been building up in the person prior to his having spoken to us. So after encouraging the person to begin, we should sit back and let him unburden himself. Initially there may be some problem, but through encouragement and patient silence, this can generally be overcome.

"The truth is, I don't know where to begin. It seems there are so many things involved, and I'm so confused."
"Jim, begin anywhere." (Long pause)
"All right, I guess I might as well start with...."

When the interaction gets going, active listening is the main technique to be employed, allowing the person to open up. We are looking for clues that might be revealed as the person's story unfolds. As the person opens up, we are to treat their material and this moment as if we were standing on "holy ground." In stage two we have been attracted to their burning issue, but now we are challenged to stay and hear their sensitive material. In the subtle (and sometimes not so subtle) messages revealed as we actively listen, a creative moment begins to emerge. The person opening up may even be surprised by the words and emotions that come. ("I didn't realize how deeply this affected me until I just said it to you.")

We will take note of any revealed clues (e.g., major topics, connecting issues, key emotional words or content, peculiar ways of saying something, our own internal reactions) for further exploration later in the conversation. Interruption at this stage is only undertaken if there is a genuine confusion on our part about what the person is saying—confusion to the extent that we would not be able to follow the person any further if we did not get immediate clarification.

As we saw in looking at the art of questioning (chapter 5), anytime we interrupt someone to ask for a point of clarification, we take a risk. By breaking in, we may be interfering with the flow of communication at a time when the person may finally be getting to some very sensitive material. So our major goals during the early phase of contact are to provide an accepting environment within which the troubled individual can open up the floodgates to the topic, to note key points in what the person is saying or how he is saying it and to note areas for further exploration once the person has completed a general overview of the issue.

Exploration

Paying attention to the material initially presented normally raises more questions than it answers. When this occurs, it is natural for the caregiver to explore further the important areas and the partially answered questions.

Selecting areas is not as difficult an undertaking as might be expected. There is no magic involved, only common sense.

Exploring further may be nothing more than seeking information that we would want if we were tackling this same problem ourselves. Our combined ability to understand the person's internal frame of reference and, also, to be outside of the interpersonal web in which he or she is caught, often gives us an ideal perspective on what may have been overlooked and needs to be explored further. Moreover, when the person tries to elaborate on techniques that have been tried, we can get an idea of the nuances in the way the problem has been handled.

Exploring further also means to go back to something that did not make sense or was quickly passed over. Often in the first telling of something important, sensitive details are omitted. When this occurs, we may scratch our heads and wonder what went wrong because in many cases the outcome seems improbable, given the approach used or the way the events were described. By questioning further and seeking additional data, the nature of the interaction that led to that outcome becomes clearer to *both* the client *and* the caregiver.

"You say she just blew up and said that she didn't want to speak to you again?"

"I couldn't believe it. I just don't know what happened."

"You said you had been just chatting with her and didn't say anything that warranted such a reaction?"

"That's right."

"Well, OK. Why don't we go back and look at the things you were saying. Maybe we can uncover something that might have ticked her off in some way without your being aware of it."

In doing this, we have to show that we are not trying to trick the person into admitting he or she did not handle things correctly. We are just looking for the truth. We are trying to perceive the situation from several different vantage points. We are making an attempt to gather *useful* information, not incriminating evidence to be used against someone.

As we explore further, we are particularly interested in those same areas we discussed in chapter 5, namely, the specific details of the situation and the feelings the person has about what happened. These feelings should include how the person felt prior to, during and after the event in question, as well as how he or she felt about what had happened, about the people involved and about the actions taken in response to the difficulty.

In the example described in chapter 4 of the mother who was upset about her daughter's suspension from school, during the initial phase the caregiver just listened to the mother relate her feelings about her daughter, the school and how her husband did not handle her daughter correctly when she was younger. A mental note was made to come back to the school suspension to get a better picture of it. There was no point in doing it when the mother was very upset and had more of a vested interest in getting her feelings out in the open than in looking more objectively at the situation. However, once the mother had an opportunity to open up, the caregiver had a chance to open up the topic of suspension.

"You say you were really upset when you heard your daughter was going to be suspended from school?"

"Yes. I felt like wringing the principal's neck. But there was nothing I could do. I just hope it doesn't keep happening. What a mess!"

Now the caregiver can seek to get a more complete view of the situation. The goal is to find out what happened and how people felt prior, during and after the event. This process is a necessary prelude to brainstorming alternatives, since without a clear understanding of what went on, little can be done in the way of problem-solving.

Alternatives

Seeking alternatives is that part of the caring exchange in which different ways of handling a problem and their possible results are explored. This stage occurs only after a fairly complete description of the factors and feelings involved has been elicited from the person who has come for care. Looking for alternatives is not easy. Although people ask for help, they often resist it because they are afraid to change. Though they want support, they do not want interference. Well-meaning help is often viewed as meddling by the very people who reach out. This is a natural pattern for most of us and should not be viewed as deceptive or hostile.

Even if the person who wants care seems unwilling to look at alternatives, at this stage of the caring exchange, at least, other factors can be introduced for consideration. Remember, the goal is not to solve the problem. That may take a lot of time. Rather, the goal is to introduce new material and open up possible avenues while supporting and accepting the person's right to feel and do what he or she thinks is best.

Remember also that in exploring alternatives we are not just looking for alternative action plans (e.g., brainstorming other things to do or say). We are also looking for alternative ways of thinking about, or seeing, a situation which, if adopted, will often change both feelings and actions. For instance, people will often have distorted thinking that intensifies emotional pain in their lives (e.g., "I really messed up on this one and now I will never be given another chance.") Exploring alternative ways of thinking will often lessen the pain (e.g., "You say you will never be given another chance, but I am wondering if there are really no circumstances under which you would be given another chance").[1]

We can also explore alternative interpretations of experiences. This is often called "reframing." A "frame" is the way we perceive an event or reality. To "reframe" an experience is to accept the facts of the situation but to see them in alternative ways.[2] For instance, people may describe times in their lives in which they feel like they are wandering, there are no answers and that they are not close to God. They are despairing because they feel God has abandoned them for some reason, and they are no longer part of the people of God. An alternative frame of interpretation might be that they are in a wilderness period like the children of Israel after they crossed the Red Sea. The wilderness is real, but God is still leading, they are still children of God, and maybe this is a part of the journey to the Promised Land.

Tying It Up

When the end of the contact is approaching, it is a good idea to try to tie things up. During this stage, there is a temptation to move quickly to fix everything and to provide advice, rather than sum up what has been covered thus far. It is as though there is a fear that unless something is done now, all will be lost.

Once I (RJW) was counseling someone with marital problems, and I saw that the session was drawing quickly to a close. Rather than wait for another meeting to methodically explore what I was thinking with him, I decided to leave him with some words of wisdom.

One of the problems I assessed was that he did not seem to be spending enough time out of the house together with his wife. So, rather than waiting until next time to explore why he was not aware of the importance of taking her out, I jumped in and said, "Maybe you should go out more often with your wife." He left without saying anything more.

The next time I saw him he greeted me with the statement: "Well, I took your *advice*." The chills went down my spine as I responded, "Oh?" He said, "Yeah. I took my wife out for dinner and while we were out someone broke into my house and stole my TV." So much for good advice.

Summarizing at the end gives a good opportunity to point out things, but it is not the time to make new strides. The end of the caring exchange is a fine time to emphasize comments and feelings that the person made with respect to important aspects of his life situation.

In reviewing these feelings and actions, the person gets another chance to see the patterns in a nutshell. The synthesis also provides a presentation of the feelings and factual content together. In this way, there is a greater chance to see the issues for what they are in the person's mind, not merely for what they appear to be on the surface.

Evaluation

A caring exchange is not really over until we take the time to evaluate what has just occurred. An array of feelings can be experienced by caregivers after the person has left and the stages of contact are over. We can walk away from the contact feeling that something positive was accomplished. On the other hand, we can feel ambivalent about the results or be convinced that the whole undertaking went sour.

Particularly when feeling discouraged, there is a need to take stock of the situation so that something can be learned from what happened. In the instances where things do not seem to go well, there is a temptation to simply blame the person who came to us. In doing this, nothing positive can result.

If we let our frustrations and bad feelings win out, we probably will think ill of the person and feel a bit disappointed in ourselves. The interaction should actually be looked upon as an opportunity to learn something positive about ourselves and the counseling process. To find out how and why things did not go as we expected, we should first ask ourselves a number of questions.

Did I expect too much from the interaction in the first place? This is the first question we should ask ourselves. In other words, did I think I could do wonders? Did I expect for some reason that this person would readily give up a lifelong style of dealing with the world? Was there some reason to believe I could fix things up overnight?

Too often we set our goals too high. We expect too much of those we deal with and see a person's willingness to open up as a sign that she or he will radically alter a familiar approach due to some advice from us.

In the first place, a caring exchange is not advice giving. If people could take advice, they probably would not need our help. Our intentional caring is designed to open up their resources so they can follow their own style of handling things, but in a way that achieves reasonable goals. Secondly, our intentional caring is based on accepting the person "as is" without trying to intrude on his or her lifestyle. This is why reflection is a major technique in caregiving. So if we are discouraged, it may be that we have failed to keep the caregiving process in its proper perspective and have expected too much from our work and supportive efforts.

This is the next question we should ask after a seemingly

unproductive session. *Did things get worse slowly or suddenly?* In answering this question we might be able to spot something we said or did that keyed a negative response in the person. This is helpful to know, not so we can castigate ourselves over our failures, but so we can see what the person is sensitive about and how we unknowingly touched this particular chord.

This self-reflection is important because it allows us to improve our style of working with others. If we can recognize the times when our intervention actually *increases* people's anxiety, we can try to work on it so the same mistake is not repeated with the person to whom we are listening or others who may have similar difficulties.

For instance, someone may be talking about her husband in a derogatory manner. We may initially bolster her by agreeing with her. However, later we may notice that she expresses guilt over having talked about her husband that way, prompting us to take steps to correct our stated misconception. Without going into the underlying dynamics of this common occurrence, suffice it to say that a caregiving principle is: Don't put yourself in a position where you are encouraging someone to be disloyal to family or friends because she will feel guilty about it afterward.

Even without knowing this principle, the same conclusion can be arrived at on our own. If we notice a negative outcome when we side with a person against family members, then we would be well advised to try not to jump in and agree with him or her the next time. Instead, we should try to get them to talk without our joining in because denunciations of family members usually turn out to be temporary. Rather than focus on the negative aspects of the person's family, we might concentrate on his or her feelings, the possible reasons why the family reacts in a specific way, and how the family may be feeling.

This is only one example of the benefits of pinpointing where a seemingly unproductive interview may have gone wrong, but it serves to illustrate the principle. It takes courage to admit you may have contributed to the negative outcome of the session, but only through this kind of self-reflection will you be able to avoid the same dangers and disappointments in the future.

Since the outcome is not what I would have liked it to be, what do I think of the person now and would I be willing to spend time helping her again? This is the final question that should be asked after an unproductive interaction. This question is important. It brings out in the open our possible frustration and anger regarding the efforts we have spent.

We might be thinking, "What a waste of time! Here she asks for help and all I get is grief for trying to be helpful." However, if we can look at the ways in which we get trapped by the other person, we can be of more use to them and others like them in the future. Also, we can begin to recognize how the people involved in the situation might feel frustrated when they deal with this person.

Do not forget, individuals who are hard to work with do not try to push people away on purpose. They may be ambivalent. Part of them wants to be heard and helped. Another part is afraid of changing and being helped. With patience and a desire to learn from our mistakes, we can continue to work with these types of people, even when others have given up. That in itself is quite an accomplishment!

With these kinds of people it is often difficult not to feel helpless and frustrated. Yet by being willing to listen and by being attentive, we may be helping them more than we realize. There are times when we think we are getting nowhere, but we are closer to the person at that moment than anyone else in the world.

They may be thinking, "Boy, she had a hard time understanding me, but at least she's interested." Such a halfhearted positive impression in their minds may be the most they can acknowledge, but the fact that they even have it is proof that our patience is worth it all.

Simply following this organizational outline gives structure to our caring exchange and facilitates our ability to be of assistance to persons in time of need. These are creative moments when we make contact, listen, problem-solve and summarize. In these moments, we join with the Spirit already moving in a person's life to **CREATE** the possibility of something new.

7. Caring for Common Problems: Depression, Anxiety and Stress

Problems, like people, come in almost every shape and size imaginable. To catalog a majority of them here, or to describe them in the context of certain stages of life, is really beyond the scope of this book and beyond what is needed by most caregivers. (For those who want to go further than what is offered here, a good resource is Joseph W. Ciarrocchi, *A Minister's Handbook of Mental Disorders.*)[1]

Some problems, however, are found often in human experience, and as caregivers we are asked to deal with them on a regular basis. Our family members, friends, neighbors or colleagues will report more often than anything feelings of sadness, insecurity or tension in their lives. They come in and say, "Boy, am I jittery. What am I going to do?" Or they look glum and report, "I just feel down all the time. I can't continue to go on like this." Or, "I feel so tense all the time. I'm under such stress. Yet, I can't seem to get out from under it all."

When these feelings are shared with us, we find ourselves on the front line of caregiving. Our response has the potential for averting a crisis or for turning a crisis into an opportunity for growth. Even if this does not happen, we can play a critical role in getting professional help for persons who present us with situations that are beyond our level of expertise.

This chapter will help us identify the common problems of depression, anxiety and stress. Identifying these common problems and learning specific ways to deal with them will help us to feel more comfortable and to focus our efforts more easily in this front line of caregiving. Furthermore, identifying these common problems will help us distinguish between their normal occurrence and their abnormal occurrence, which, in the case of the latter, may call for a referral to a professional (see chapter 9).

Depression

Identifying the problem. Most of us are familiar with a number of signs of depression. Yet other signs are not so familiar because on first blush they may not appear to be related to depression. Signs of depression fall into four categories: emotions or feelings, behavior, physiology and thoughts. Our task is to be aware of these signs so that we might recognize them when they are mentioned to us, but also so that we might ask the right questions when we are encouraging a person to elaborate upon his or her story.

Not all depressed people who come to us will say that they are depressed. An individual may come with a story of marital discord. Another may come with a story of how life is changing now that he is retired, or a child has been born, or a child has left home or that some other life transition has occurred. Someone else may tell us that every year at the same time she cannot find the energy to do normal tasks. Others may come with stories of guilt and spiritual struggle. By listening and asking the right questions, we may discover that they are depressed.

Remembering the four categories for signs of depression, we will want to ask how the person is *feeling emotionally.* How a person answers this question will be quite varied. Someone can be upset, feeling blue, angry, agitated, happy, OK, blah, worried, fearful, excited or any other of a number of things. To answer this question and determine what the person's mood level is, we should ask the person to report personal feeling levels, or we should point out our observations ("You seem really down"). This should enable us to start an open discussion in this area.

Feelings that indicate depression are feelings of being blue, "down in the dumps," sad or irritable.

We will want to inquire about the person's *behavior* if we suspect depression. A person with depression will often have a loss of interest or pleasure in activities they once enjoyed. A person who once got excited about gardening as a hobby may report having no desire to plant a thing this year and, instead, may feel like plowing everything under. Other persons will report a loss of interest in sex or a loss of appetite. Others may report binge eating and weight gain. Changes in sleeping patterns may also be noted. Some people will want to stay in bed all day, unable to face the world and not feel rested after many hours of sleep. Others may report being unable to fall asleep, waking up repeatedly at night, or waking up one to two hours early each day and not being able to go back to sleep.

Physiology, or bodily symptoms, are also an area of inquiry. Restlessness or retarded movement and speech may indicate depression. Often bodily aches and pains are reported for which no medical causes can be found. Headaches, stomachaches, cold symptoms or feeling sore all over may point to a psychological ache as well. While we obviously should not play physician with people, such physical complaints can tip us off to the possible presence of emotional ailments. Emotional depression and minor physical ailments are often present simultaneously. Asking a person whether he has discussed the generally poor way he feels with a physician can open the topic. Sometimes a person who has previously avoided discussing his general malaise with a doctor may be willing to talk about it now.

The nature of a person's *thoughts* may also indicate signs of depression. A person may have difficulty remembering things, concentrating or making decisions. A person may have thoughts of helplessness, worthlessness and hopelessness. Aaron Beck says that there are three major thought patterns that are distorted in a depressed person.[2] The depressed person views events, themselves and the future in negative ways. Events that others see as positive or neutral the depressed person will see as failures or "not good enough." The depressed person will view his or her self as guilty or worse than others. The future looks bleak and full of pain to the depressed person.

The depressed person may also have thoughts of suicide. About 15 percent of depressed persons eventually do commit suicide. Therefore, as caregivers we need to take all talk about killing oneself seriously. Sometimes suicidal thoughts will be passive ("I had the feeling that I wanted to run my car off the road coming home"). Other thoughts will be more specific ("I have a gun I keep loaded in the car, and I know a quiet road where no one will hear if I blow my brains out"). If we encourage the person to talk about the possibility of suicide, will we not be putting the thought in his or her head? On the contrary, we will be helping them find relief in talking about it and will be better able to assess the lethal nature of the person's thinking. In every case, it is imperative to get professional help for someone who is feeling suicidal. The more specific and potentially lethal their plans, the more quickly we need to get them to professional help, being careful not to leave them alone.

Everyone will feel some of the above symptoms from time to time. As caregivers we can distinguish between the normal "blues" and abnormal depression by the severity of the symptoms, the length of time the symptoms have been manifested and how incapacitating the symptoms are for a person. A person who has felt down for a couple of days and has gone to work with a little less energy is different from someone who, for the past couple of weeks, has found nothing good in life and has not been able to get out of bed on a regular basis to go to work.

Ways to help. As we make contact with people, look for revelations and get them to elaborate on what is bothering them, we are already helping the situation by allowing them to express, or vent, their emotions. During this phase of our caring exchange, we are in a good position to help a person deal with the *expression of anger.* Pent-up anger is a major psychological cause of depression. People sit on their anger for many reasons (none the least of which is that many people feel that anger is not an acceptable emotion), and when they do, it can lead to feelings of remorse, ineffectuality and self-deprecation. Recognizing anger and identifying the reasons for it is an important step in helping the depressed person. The tip-off to the presence of such anger is that the person seems to assume all of the responsibility for a problem. The following conversation shows how anger can be recognized and examined.

"What's the matter, Toni?"

"I just can't seem to handle Mom. She's been so good to me all these years, but I find that I treat her horribly. She's so sweet. Her treatment of me and the kids is all in my best interest and theirs, but I get so upset with her. I wish I wouldn't blow off the handle that way."

"What's been going on recently between the two of you?"

"Well, last night I told the boys they could stay up another half hour. I really didn't think they should have, but they were being good and I'd rather they sit and watch TV quietly than fight in their bedroom."

"And?"

"Well, when Mom walked in she told them to go to bed and she started hounding them. They got upset. Then she came to me and told me I was spoiling them and that they had answered her back, so I had no choice but to punish them by sending them to bed. What a mess. Well, at any rate, I told her I was tired of her meddling and she got angry at me and stormed up to bed. I went up and apologized, but she wouldn't even talk to me. When Jack finally came home from the evening shift, I was all in tears. He got angry at me and my mother and, well, it just made the whole thing worse. I'm just a failure with everyone it seems" (crying).

"You seem really down on yourself."

"Well, I never seem to do anything right. I guess I do spoil the kids, and I don't raise them as well as mother could, but I do my best."

"What does Jack think?"

"He thinks I should tell my mother off, but I love her. I'm bad enough to her as it is. I ought to be nicer."

"You say you're bad to her. Can you explain how you were bad to her in the incident last night?"

"Well, I shouldn't have told her to stop meddling. They are her grandchildren. And she was right."

"How were you feeling when you told her to stop meddling?"

"I was angry, I mean annoyed that she got them worked up."

"So you were angry because you felt she got them worked up?"

"Well, I realize I'm wrong in that now. She was right, of course. I do spoil them."

"That's another issue. You were angry at her because she got them worked up. How did that occur?"

"Well, as I said. I had told them one thing and she then told them another, and they got upset and confused."

"Do you think that's good for them?"

"No. That's what bothers me. I don't think it's good for them to have more than Jack and me telling them what to do, especially after I've told them one thing and she tells them another. They're losing respect for me and I'm losing control of them."

"So, you were angry at your mother for interfering. Even if she has the children's best interest at heart, you were thinking they're your children and you're responsible for raising them."

"Yes, but she means well."

"A lot of people who mean well make mistakes."

"But I don't want her to think I don't love her."

"What would make her think that?"

"Well, if I get angry at her, wouldn't she feel that way?"

"Well, you continue to get angry at her now because you don't believe she should interfere with the way you raise your children. But you don't express it when you're calm—only after a problem has occurred. Instead of letting the resentment build, how do you think you could tell your mom not to give your children orders countermanding yours?"

"That's just it. If I say something about her interfering, she gets hurt. Nothing I say seems right."

"Well, it seems you tell her only when you're distraught. Also, maybe your mother needs to be told constantly until it gets through. Otherwise, it seems your children will continue to suffer and so will you and Jack."

"But she'll feel I'm blaming her for all my problems."

"Are you?"

"No. Though sometimes I feel we'd be better without her meddling."

"If you feel that way, then you must be angry at her interference. You also must be convinced she is causing problems."

"I am."

"Then you have to talk to her to at least open the question. If you're afraid of her rejection of you because of it, then recall your priorities and the goal you have in bringing up the topic with her."

"What do you mean?"

"Well, you and your husband have the responsibility to raise your children, just as your mother had the responsibility for raising you and your brothers. This doesn't mean you're rejecting your mother, but rather you are setting things straight. Also, if you let her know how you feel when you're not angry, she can't accuse you of trying to lash out at her. If she does, then it's her problem. Since she is your mother you can help her with it, but not at the expense of your children."

"That's easier said than done."

"That's right, but it's a beginning."

The above interaction has been compressed for purposes of space here. In reality, Toni would do a lot more of the talking and the caregiver would be a good deal less directive. However, this vignette does show a number of points on dealing with a depressed person who is trying to hide or suppress the anger present.

The anger must be opened up to see why it is not coming out more directly. In Toni's case, it may be because she fears rejection by her mother and at the same time doubts her ability to raise her children. In addition, she may bottle up her anger because she fears that expressing it directly would be so devastating that she might do something outrageous that she would regret. The goal is to get the anger out in the open to show that it is there. The next step is to demonstrate that one doesn't have to deal with an unsatisfactory situation out of anger, but that reasonable measures can be taken in the hope of improving the situation for all concerned.

One factor evident in people's inability to deal with anger in a healthy way is their inability to distinguish between assertion and aggression. Many people think that if they experience anger and act upon it, they are behaving aggressively, and that others will think ill of them for it. But it is possible to recognize anger and then to act in a calm, assertive way intended to alleviate a situation. Assertive statements are clear, firm and to the point. Assertive statements are the healthy middle ground between being passive (saying nothing) and being aggressive (blowing up at someone). Assertive statements are expressions of powerful love. By helping people sort out the differences among anger, aggression and assertion in the actions they take, the purposes they have and the way they handle others (who themselves may mistakenly equate assertion with aggression), it is possible to help people deal with their problems more directly.

We can further help the depressed person when, in our caring exchange, we come to look at alternatives. Many depressed persons need to explore *alternatives to their helplessness,* since helplessness is another major psychological cause for depression.

Helplessness occurs when our coping mechanisms appear temporarily out of order. This can occur for any number of reasons. A situation may be very new to us, and we may be temporarily overwhelmed. We may have reached a point in our lives where we need to alter our goals. We may need to be a little more patient with others, ourselves and the situation: *when* we do something is just as important as what we do. The potential causes of helplessness go on and on.

There are a number of things we can do for people once we observe that the feeling of helplessness is a central issue. Among them are:

1. Demonstrate a willingness to listen to their concerns about being ineffectual.
2. Help them achieve goal clarification.
3. Participate in a problem-solving operation.
4. Provide support for the belief that things will improve (if, in fact, this is true).
5. Show a desire to look at current thinking patterns.

The following vignette shows how a caregiver can help a person who feels helpless and depressed. In this typical situation, a young woman is speaking with her father concerning the problem of finding employment.

"What's the matter, Hon?"

"You wasted your money, Dad. You wasted one big chunk of your money."

"So, what else is old?"

"No, I'm not kidding."

"What are you talking about?"

"Sending me to school. It was all a waste."

"Having a hard time with finding a job, eh?"

"I've been pounding the pavement. I'm sick of it. It's the same old garbage. Each job I apply for requires previous experience. How are you supposed to get experience if you can't get a job? I think I was born too late. I should have come along when they were giving positions away."

"I don't remember those days."

"You know what I mean. This is serious. What am I going to do? The situation really seems hopeless."

"What kind of positions are you looking for?"

"Anything. Believe me anything!"

"When we feel hopeless and a bit desperate, it's natural to feel the way you do. I can understand and accept it, Carol, but it won't help you to get a job."

"Then what do you suggest?"

"Before I go into the suggestion business, let's see why you feel so hopeless. I think that's one of your main stumbling blocks. You're already very upset and feel all is lost."

"I just can't help it."

"What do you mean?"

"Well I've tried so many things. I'm just ready to give up. That's all."

"Well, sit down. Let's see what you've tried. Tell me what you've been doing to get a job."

"Well, I listed myself with the college placement bureau. I told them I was interested in a job in advertising. Then I've answered ads in the paper for ad assistants, but without any luck. Finally, out of desperation, I went to three employment agencies and they said all they had were secretarial positions. Finally, I started knocking on doors of companies in the city to see if anything was open. The result was a big fat zero. So, what else am I supposed to do? I really think I've done all I can."

"What made you decide on advertising?"

"Well, my major is English. I can't think of any other interesting field where I could use it. In desperation, though, I told the agencies I would do anything, so it's not as though I'm not open to suggestions."

"And they responded?"

"Well, they said I was unskilled, so I would have a hard time finding something."

"So, on the one hand, you looked for advertising jobs, but when things didn't seem to be open, you told potential employers you would work in any area."

"You think that was a mistake?"

"Well, it seems that on the one hand you're looking for a very specialized position, and on the other you are possibly giving them the impression that you don't know what you want to do."

"Well, what do you think I should have done?"

"I don't know. I'm not an English major. However, there should be someone who could help you narrow down the types of jobs and traineeships you might apply for, given your broad background."

"Like who?"

"Are there people in your school, either in the English department or the placement or guidance offices, who can be of help?"

"There might be, but I doubt it."

"But it's one avenue of approach, eh?"

"Yes, I guess you're right. Still, I think I'm going to need a contact the way the job market is today, no matter what you say."

"What makes you think I don't feel that the idea of a contact is a good one?"

"Didn't you just say I should go to the school and ask them for help?"

"Right, but I think your ideas will turn out to be the best. You know your situation better than anyone. I believe, however, you would do best to approach the job problem on a number of fronts. After all, didn't you say getting a job was going to be a problem?"

"A killer."

"Fine. So, you go to the school. We'll sit down and discuss what contacts we might have in the family and among our friends later tonight when your mother's home from work."

"But we don't know anyone in advertising, do we?"

"Probably not, but we may know people in allied areas—ones suggested by people at your school—that may give you a start. Remember, if you take a position, it doesn't have to be one you're so thrilled with that you have to stay in it all of your life. After all, the experience

is an issue; they're big on it in business even if it's not in a related area."

"I hadn't thought of that. You know, I feel a bit better. At least I have a few things to work on. Maybe something will turn up."

"I'm glad you feel better. We'll do everything in our power to make *something turn up. We'll look at a number of options to see what is really open to you without being too specialized or general, OK?"*

"Sure. Thanks a lot."

In the example, the listener set the atmosphere in a way that was relaxed and open. The young woman felt it was all right to vent her frustrations and feelings of impotence. When this was done, an effort to clarify immediate goals and develop steps for solving the problem at hand were undertaken. Finally, after the airing of feelings and mutual problem-solving, a look was taken at her current thinking patterns.

As can be seen, there is nothing magical in helping someone. But neither was this intervention mere purposeless interaction that anyone could do. In a brief conversation, for instance, the father might have been tempted to jump in early in the game and give his daughter a sugar-coated pep talk: "Hey, don't worry, things will work out. It's nothing." The implication of such a response is, "I don't want to listen to this; it makes me feel uncomfortable and helpless. Please go away and come back when things are better so I can say, 'See, I told you things would work out.' "

In light conversation where people do not involve themselves in problem-solving with the person in need, the temptation is to provide a pat solution. In giving pat solutions, though, we risk taking away the independence of the other individual, and it seems like we are trying to push our answers onto the other person. This usually fails to be of any help to the person because people are different and have different goals and styles of coping.

In the conversation between father and daughter, the father also demonstrated ideal caring skills. First, he had a good deal of patience with his daughter. Not only did he encourage her to open up, but he did not lash out when she expressed irritability and a sense of global futility about what they were discussing. Neither did he march in paternally and attempt to offer the golden key to solving the problem. Rather, he sought to work with her on developing her own avenues of approach.

In tying the problem down to specific approaches, the daughter's overall feeling of helplessness started to diminish. There was hope—hope based on the perception that there was a way out. This is very important, since people often feel that they have tried everything and the situation is generally hopeless with no real way out unless a break comes along or something happens to them.

This passive waiting for something to happen can become quite serious. It is based on the belief that the person cannot do anything or initiate actions, and it encourages a passive outlook. A vicious circle can result if someone does not have the patience to demonstrate a belief in the person's coping powers while problem-solving with him.

The emphasis in dealing with the depressed person who feels helpless is on *patience.* Depressed people can be most irritating. They seem to want help, but when we reach out they may seem to indicate that our efforts on their behalf are foolish or not good enough. This can arouse a good deal of anger in us if their resistance is not anticipated and pointed out in a nonangry way.

The best way to deal with potential resistance is to keep in mind a number of points prior to and during your interaction with the person. These points can be summarized as follows:

1. We can help them most by being patient, supportive and not quickly dismissing their expressions of helplessness and anger.

2. In most cases, the real difficulty lies not so much in the problems that they bring up, but rather in their *perceptions* of the problems and the negative ways that they view their coping abilities. Therefore, we should not try to jump in and solve the problems, but should methodically support their renewed, sensible efforts to cope.

3. Just because people do not leave us feeling super does not mean we have failed to help them. To think so might make us not want to try to help them in the future when, in fact, this would be the worst thing we could do. If we are willing to accept

people's rights to feel down at times, they will recognize this and come back with renewed hope that someone cares.

4. Depressed people are often down because of erroneous, all-encompassing messages they give themselves. "There is nothing I can do," "I feel so futile," "I guess I'll just have to wait until something happens," "I guess it is just God's will for me to be this way," are all global, negative messages. Part of the effort we make with depressed people centers on questioning these messages. Ask them why a particular failure means that there is nothing they can do in a situation, or why they see a particular bit of bad luck as evidence that their lives are going wrong. Point out the distortion of such expectations and thinking patterns and then have them go over the steps they have taken and the feelings they have experienced.

Often depressed people will think that they are "bad," or that they lack faith or that God is punishing them for something they have done wrong. We need to hear that pain and not minimize the feelings. However, when we come to look at alternative ways of thinking, we can, for example, interject the thought that Elijah seemed to be depressed and suicidal at times (1 Kings 19:4), or that Job was certainly down. Many religious figures at times of growth have experienced "dark nights of the soul" or "wilderness periods" in their lives, which may not be the same as clinical depression, but may have something of the same feel. Well-known historical figures have experienced depression. Winston Churchill, for example, experienced recurring depression, which he referred to as his "black friend." Abraham Lincoln experienced such marked drops in mood that he feared carrying a gun in case the temptation to commit suicide might be too great to resist. Depression can be present in any type of person—rich, poor, young, elderly, Caucasian, Chicano, unemployed, business executive, politician or religious leader. No group is exempt.

Sometimes the thoughts of being "bad" or lacking faith are intensified when it is decided that a depressed person really needs to take medication for his or her depression. Of course, we will not make that decision, but someone to whom we have referred a depressed person may recommend medication. Often the depressed person will come back to us as a trusted friend and ask, "Should I take this? Won't it mess up my mind? Will it make me somebody different than who I am? Shouldn't I just rely upon God to help me get over this?" Again, after hearing his or her dilemma, we can play a crucial role as caregivers by suggesting alternative ways of thinking. We can suggest that they will still be in control of their lives, that taking this kind of medication does not question their faith anymore than taking any other medication (like antibiotics), and that God has given us science, too, which is a powerful tool when used in combination with one's faith.

Related issues. For some persons there is a swing from being really down and depressed to "flying high" in an intense euphoric mood. The mood of euphoria may be accompanied by dramatic increases in energy, rapid and pressured speech, increased interest in sex and poor judgment, resulting in shopping sprees or risky financial investments. Such a person is not merely suffering from depression, but from bipolar disorder as well (formerly called manic-depression), and needs to be referred immediately to a professional for help.

Codependency is a very popular term that has to do with a form of relating to others that becomes self-defeating or destructive. Often this can lead to depressed feelings, but the depressed feelings are not necessarily continuous. Rather, the depressed feelings will follow the ups and downs of the relationship, and the primary issue is a way of relating to significant others that does not incorporate a balance between attachment to and separation from the other person. Codependent relationship is defined by one author as, "...one in which an individual defines herself or himself primarily in terms of the other person. Codependent persons have little sense of meaning or value in their own life except that which comes through this relationship, around which they focus all of their energy. Without the relationship, codependent people are afraid they would have no sense of self."[3] Codependent persons need to recover (rather than depress) their own feelings, likes and dislikes, sense of direction, et cetera, which are independent of the other person and which can be expressed while still being close to that other person. A number of popular books are available to help people work through issues of codependency.[4]

Grief is not the same thing as depression, even though the grieving person can often exhibit signs of depression. Grief is the result of a loss, which, for example, can include the loss of another person, the loss of a job or the loss of property. If the depressed feelings resulting from the loss are intense and continue for more than two months after the loss, we might consider this as a case of depression rather than grief. Grieving people often have periods of depression that come and go, usually tapering off in intensity over time. A depressed person usually has depressed feelings almost all of the time that continue for weeks, months or even years.[5]

Grief is ordinary and experienced by all human beings at some time or another. Grief confronts us with the power of loss and forces us to redefine our inner images that help us to cope with reality.[6] Andrew Lester suggests that grief is a loss of our "future stories," which we have constructed to give our lives a sense of direction.[7] A mother who always thought that her youngest son would take care of her in old age lived with that inner image, or future story, until her son was killed. In her grief work she had to construct another story about her future that no longer included the youngest son. Until she came up with a new "future story," she could not hope.

Anxiety

Identifying the problem. Throughout classical Greek literature, we see references to the sin of "hubris" (excessive behavior). To the Greeks of that era, excess in any form was wrong. They constantly emphasized and encouraged all to live in line with the golden mean. Hubris refers to excesses in either direction. Too little was just as bad as too much; starvation and gluttony were equally horrible.

Anxiety works the same way—too little can be as bad as too much. If we are overly anxious, we will suffer notably. On the other hand, if we feel no anxiety whatsoever about our current efforts and future aspirations, our motivation will probably shrivel and dry up.

Anxiety has a place in our lives. However, the role it plays is a precarious one. If it becomes too predominant, it stifles the very activity it would normally facilitate. This has been shown to be the case among college students preparing for exams. When almost no anxiety is present, the student is not apt to prepare well. Slight anxiety regarding performance on a test is a positive factor. When students are a bit worried about how they will fare, they tend to work harder to ensure good results. When the anxiety becomes too great, though, the motivation to study becomes thwarted. The student who is very worried about the outcome becomes so upset that the worrying interferes with his studying. Efforts at mastering the material are supplanted by feelings of, "What's the use; I'll never get it now. It's too late!"

Anxiety is tied to our ability to think about and plan the future through problem-solving and learning ways to cope with the uncertainties of life. For this reason, one researcher has called anxiety the "shadow of intelligence."

Most people who come to us for care will not be coming because they have too little anxiety in their lives. However, we can be alert for this possibility when we listen and hear of a person being unable to get motivated for a job or being too relaxed about an important upcoming event. If we detect too little anxiety in the situation, we might help them explore such causes as overconfidence, a denial of anxiety (manifesting itself, for example, as a show of bravado by a person who finds feelings of insecurity too unbearable), ignorance of the complexity or demands of a situation and apathy. Apathy usually results from previously unrewarding experiences concerning the anxiety-provoking situation. The person may have tried everything to ward off his or her anxious feelings and met with no results, or the person may have been so overanxious that withdrawal seemed the only reasonable alternative.

Most people who come to us for care will be coming because of too much anxiety in their lives rather than too little. All of us have a certain degree of anxiety about living when we think about our jobs, finances, relationships, families, health or safety.

What distinguishes abnormal anxiety from normal anxiety is the duration of the anxiety, the intensity of the symptoms and the likelihood of a particular worrisome event actually happening.

Anxiety is basically fear, but it is fear in reaction to a vague or indirect threat as opposed to a direct threat. Being confronted by an angry, dangerous animal would be a direct threat and would produce fear. Living in a corporate world with rumors of job elimination and downsizing is (at least at the rumor stage) an indirect threat that could produce a lot of daily anxiety as a person wondered about job security.

With increased levels of anxiety, persons may report to us feelings of fear or dread accompanied by feelings of tension, dizziness, irritability, tightness in the chest and inability to stop worrying. We may observe in such persons trembling, shaking, twitching, pacing, being easily startled and difficulty sleeping. Other signs of anxiety are rapid heartbeat, sweating, frequent urination, nausea, dry mouth, clammy hands, "lump in the throat" and hot or cold flashes.

There are many possible causes of anxiety. For some, it seems to stem from a genetic predisposition. While some persons are predisposed to respond to life's uncertainties with depression, others are predisposed to respond with anxiety. There are possible biological causes for anxiety resulting from the excessive production of arousal neurotransmitters in the nervous system.

Sometimes there are "underlying" causes for anxiety. Some theorists suggest that there are unconscious, unacceptable thoughts that create a free-floating anxiety that will attach to particular events in life. Others suggest that anxiety can be attributed to something real or imagined that stirs up fears of loss of control, retaliation, physical injury or separation. A person who fears losing control is afraid that "letting go" will result in aggressive or antisocial behavior. Jane, for instance, was constantly anxious around her mother. As she talked through her concerns, it was finally determined that Jane was fearful of losing control and acting out physically against her mother and that she was also afraid of being beaten up by her mother. Such anxiety had roots in earlier childhood fears and traumas, which is also often the source of anxieties about physical injury or separation.

Other causes of anxiety include faulty or maladaptive thinking. Anxious people will often leap to illogical conclusions, think only about the worst possible outcomes, assume that life will turn out badly for them and forget about their own abilities to respond to life's events. Changing their thinking will often result in a lowering of their anxiety.

Ways to help. As we make contact with a person, seek revelation and help her to elaborate on her problem, we are already beginning to help the anxious person by enabling her to express her feelings and put words to her specific anxiety. This begins to make the fear less vague or diffuse by bringing it into clear focus.

In this stage of our intentional conversation, we will want to understand the person's unique fears (which may seem unwarranted from our perspective) and stand with him in the anxiety. At this point, there are two mistakes to avoid—namely, jumping in too quickly with reassurance and allowing ourselves to get trapped by the other person's anxiety. Quick reassurances may alleviate the anxiety of the caregiver, but it can actually increase the anxiety of the one who is seeking care. For example, Lisa talked with her friend about her fears of financial security. She had a steady job that paid reasonably well, but she had daily anxiety about her ability to afford a car if her present one stopped running or how she would ever afford to buy a house on her current income level. Her friend merely said that she once had those fears but grew out of them and that, as the scriptures promised, God would take care of her if she would just stop worrying about it all. Lisa left the encounter feeling that there was something really wrong with her because she could not do this, which only increased her anxiety.

Getting caught up in the other person's anxiety is another pitfall to avoid at this stage of the caring exchange. Anxious people may tend not to hear what we are saying. They may project their anger onto us at the same time that they are reaching out to us, or they may make us anxious through the ways they act or through their expressions of nervousness. If we can keep our own feelings in check and try to support the person while attempting to tie his or her anxiety to something concrete, the results can be quite positive.

As we move to help anxious people look at alternatives, it is best to help them establish a procedure for being concrete about the anxiety, about their assumptions in response to the anxiety and about their abilities to cope with what they fear will happen. It is most helpful to get people in the habit of writing about their anxieties. Any time they are anxious, they are to take a sheet of paper and write in one column what is specifically making them anxious. In the next column they can write an assessment of how anxious they are (on a scale of 0 to 100). In the next column, they are to write down their automatic thoughts, which include their assumptions about how things will turn out. In the next column, they are to write other possible outcomes and other more rational ways of thinking their responses and abilities to cope. In the final column, they are to again assess their anxieties on a scale of 0 to 100 to see whether these feelings have actually lessened.

Mike would often wake up with a high degree of anxiety about his work. In a time of recession, his business had not done well, and he had borrowed some money from friends to keep the business going until the economy turned around. The economy was turning around, but this did not help Mike's anxiety. Each morning he was anxious about what would happen in the business.

As he began to be concrete about his anxiety, Mike wrote in the first column that what he really feared was that his friend would come through the door, ask for his money, and that he wouldn't have the cash to repay. He rated his anxiety at 85. In the next column, he wrote his assumptions that his friend would be angry in demanding the money and threaten to sue him or ruin his reputation. In the next column, Mike began to write that it was really unlikely that his friend would be that angry, even if he did demand his money. It was unlikely that his friend would sue him. At the same time, he began to think of how he could get the money if he had to do so. He did not like all the alternatives, but he could see a progression of steps he could take. Even if the worst happened and he had to sell his house, he was able to think that God would show him a way to survive and that he would probably feel even closer to God since the anxiety would be out of his way. Finally, Mike again rated his anxiety and found that it had dropped to 25. He could now get on with his day and be more productive in his business, which, in the long run, would help him get out of debt.

This structured way of writing about one's anxieties helps to make the fear behind the anxiety less vague or diffuse. More complete instructions for this approach can be found in a number of popular books.[8] In addition to this structured way of writing, some people find it helpful to write more generally in a journal asking such questions as, "Where is God asking me to grow in all of this?" Again, a number of popular books can expand one's knowledge of what to ask and what to write.[9]

It is also helpful to encourage anxious persons to learn some form of relaxation. This can be done by learning some form of muscle relaxation in which a person alternately tenses and then relaxes each muscle group from the head to the toes. Relaxation can also be incorporated into a person's daily prayer time. For instance, while breathing calmly, a person can say over and over the ancient prayer of the church: "Lord, Jesus Christ (breathe in calmly), have mercy on me (breathe out calmly)." While remembering to breathe calmly, other persons find it helpful to recite a favorite passage of scripture such as, "I can do all things through Christ who strengthens me" (Philippians 4:13).

Related issues. In all cases we can be of help by assessing the severity of anxiety and getting a person to a professional if the level of anxiety is intense. It is also important for us to be aware of special anxiety situations that require the attention of a professional. Some persons have particular phobias, which are fears of particular objects or experiences that present no real harm to the individual or such low danger that other persons would ignore it. Fear of certain animals (like snakes or dogs), fear of flying or fear of social situations can create intense anxiety in certain people, causing them to need professional attention.

Other persons experience intense spells or attacks of anxiety when nothing harmful is present. Panic attacks seem to come from nowhere, may cause a person to feel like he or she will lose control by fainting, dying or going crazy. People with panic attacks often learn to avoid certain locations that they associate with these unpredictable and uncontrollable episodes. Again, the help of a professional is in order when we assess that a person is suffering from panic attacks.

Finally, some persons will tell us of anxious behavior that is compulsive in nature. People may wash their hands over and over in order to diminish a fear of germs, or they may check that they locked the doors over and over again before they can leave the house or go to sleep. Religious compulsions can include ritualistic prayers repeated for thirty to sixty minutes in order to atone for some "bad" thought, or having to touch the Bible and recite certain scriptures to prevent the death of a loved one. Compulsions are ways of reducing anxiety created by repulsive, intrusive thoughts (obsessions). Thoughts of having committed the "unforgivable sin," having a thought that one might kill another accidentally, or thoughts of participating in some sexual act, can be obsessions. We can be of great help in noticing the compulsive actions of some persons, listening to their obsessive thinking (if they will tell us), and helping them find their way to a professional for treatment of this disorder.[10]

Stress

Identifying the problem. The upsets people experience, including their manifestation of depression and anxiety, are often caused by unhealthy amounts of stress. The more we know about stress, the better we can help others and be able to avoid its unpleasant effects ourselves.

Stress can take many forms and arise in a number of surprising ways. In some cases stress is hard to identify, and its immediate causes difficult to pinpoint. Like depression and anxiety, it can be serious or minor, brief or long lasting, observable and external, or unconscious and internal in origin. Some stress, like anxiety, is necessary for life because it enables us to cope with potentially demanding factors that continually confront us.

The basic source of stress is *change.* Stress results when an organism attempts to adapt to a change in its environment. Too many assignments on the job, a death in the family, an appointment with someone we want to impress, a move to a new area can all be sources of stress. Similarly, a buildup of *little* irritants or daily hassles (like an uncooperative spouse, having to fight traffic, or a noisy neighbor) and even what we eat cause stress in our lives.

Stress can arise from happy events in our lives just as much as from unhappy ones. It is true that the happy events may, in the end, put less pressure on us overall, but the important thing to note is that it is change—any change—that is the root of stress.

In biological terms, stress is a state of readiness. When it gets the message that something is a stressor, the brain sends alarm messages that prepare the body for fight or flight. If we were attacked by an intruder, we might respond by fighting or fleeing, but the body's reaction would be the same either way, as muscles tighten, senses heighten and heart and breathing rates increase. Such a state of readiness is to our advantage for survival. It only becomes a problem when we are in a state of readiness for prolonged periods of time due to constant stressors around us or due to our peculiar perception of events around us that we interpret as threatening. The stress resulting from a prolonged state of readiness can take its toll on our bodies and can even contribute to the process of aging.

In spiritual terms, stress can be thought of as a call to wake up: to take a closer look at the way we are living our lives, or the way we think about life; to take a closer look at our inner selves; to take a closer look at our spiritual health. Perhaps we are being called in the stress of life to wake up to the fact that we have wandered too far from the "still waters" of the Good Shepherd, or that we have refused the leading of God, who would restore our soul.[11]

The signs of stress are numerous. The Hungarian physician, Hans Selye, who spent a lifetime studying stress, developed the following comprehensive list: (1) general irritability, hyperexcitation or depression; (2) pounding of the heart; (3) dryness of the throat and mouth; (4) impulsive behavior, emotional instability; (5) the overpowering urge to cry or run and hide; (6) inability to concentrate; (7) feelings of unreality, weakness or dizziness; (8) feelings of fatigue and the loss of the joy of living; (9) floating anxiety; (10) emotional tension and alertness; (11) trembling, nervous ticks; (12) tendency to be easily startled; (13) high-pitched, nervous laughter; (14) stuttering and other speech problems; (15) grinding of the teeth; (16) insomnia; (17) hypermobility; (18) sweating; (19) frequent need to urinate; (20) diarrhea, indigestion; (21) migraine headaches; (22) premenstrual tension or missed menstrual cycles; (23) pain in the neck or lower back; (24) loss of or excessive appetite; (25) increased smoking; (26) increased use of illegally prescribed drugs; (27) alcohol and drug addiction; (28) nightmares; (29) neurotic behavior; (30) psychoses; (31) accident proneness.[12]

Ways to help. As we help people elaborate their stories and move on to look at alternatives, we will want to keep in mind the following general questions to guide us:

1. When did the person first start to feel pressured?

2. What can be done to recognize potentially hazardous patterns like this in the future?

3. How can one deal with stress when it first appears, prevent it from getting greater and actually reduce it?

4. What factors in a person make one more susceptible to stress?

5. What alternatives are open now and in the future to help one enjoy change that is pleasant and deal with change that is not?

6. What are the possible supports that can be mustered internally and in the outer environment to help in the handling of stress?

These are general principles that become specific and useful when a person comes to us under pressure. As we problem-solve with them, they should be able to work on developing a better style of handling pressure. The goal is to make them see what specifically led to their being unprepared for stress, unable to reduce it and presently unable to learn from the mistakes they made.

For example, Aaron complained that the world seemed to be caving in for him, that he was being pulled in a million directions and was feeling terrible as well. On the job, which was at its seasonal high, the work was demanding, complex and required a good deal of time on the job site as well as a good deal of thought when he was home, supposedly resting. His family felt neglected and was angry that he could not spend more time with them. It was coming to the end of the two-month busy period; they had had it and they told him so. Now he had gotten a bad cold and was feeling physically exhausted. He expressed the feeling that he was failing in every role—father, husband, provider, employee, supervisor and mature person in control.

In working with Aaron, discussion of how he got into this situation proved quite fruitful in planning for when the busy season would return next year. Exploring how he might settle things with his family and distance himself for short periods of time when away from the job seemed to deflate the immediate pressures and feelings of loss of control that were plaguing him. In other words, by focusing on the development of the problem and the priorities that could be designed, Aaron felt the power of knowledge and control again. This, in turn, helped him to deal more effectively with those factors that he had previously just viewed as part of his problem.

In addition to these general principles, it is helpful in dealing with persons under stress to remember that stress can come from one's body, environment, relationships and thinking. If we can reduce the stress in any one of these areas, we can often reduce the overall stress in a person's life, even if a primary stressor cannot be immediately eliminated. Those people who are experiencing stress from their jobs and cannot change the situations in the short run can make sure their bodies are healthy, eliminate other hassles in their lives, strengthen primary relationships and challenge their own thoughts about a situation.

Our *bodies* can become increasingly stress resistant by watching our diets, getting proper sleep, exercising and learning relaxation techniques. We can build a reserve of energy in our bodies that helps us cope with stress when things get pressured.

We can reduce stress in our *environments* by noticing even little things that irritate us and by treating ourselves to improvements. We can rearrange our schedules so that there are spaces to take a deep breath and center ourselves. We can paint drab walls or arrange our living quarters for greater efficiency. We can also work to channel our money and our time toward our own personal goals in life, simplifying and eliminating expenditures and activities that are not contributing to where we want to go in life.

Our *relationships* can either create stress or help to eliminate stress. To eliminate stress in our relationships, we need to work on proper boundaries without setting up barriers that totally keep other people out. Those with proper boundaries can invite people to be close but are not afraid to say "no" when they feel invaded or taken advantage of. They use the language of assertiveness, which is the healthy middle ground between saying nothing (even if they are hurt) and going to the other extreme of being aggressive (attacking with harsh words or increased volume).

Our *thinking* will often affect whether or not we experience stress in any given circumstance. What one person sees as stressful is not stressful at all to another person. Individual differences, including how we think about particular events, are usually the determining factors. Epictetus wrote, "Men are disturbed not by things but by the views which they take of things." Shakespeare wrote, "There is nothing good or bad, but thinking makes it so." Even before these writers, it was written in Proverbs 23:7, "As a man thinketh in his heart, so is he." As we care for others who are under stress, we can help them explore alternative thoughts. Often it is good to get people to write down what it is that is pressuring them and then to write down their thoughts that come automatically. Next, they can look at other thoughts and possible outcomes as well as evaluate the ways they could cope, even if the worst possible outcome happened.

Stress provides the opportunity for us to evaluate our lives in many areas. Stress can be a wake-up call that forces us to look at our destructive life patterns and that enables us to find within us and beyond us resources to cope with a changing world.

Related issues. Burnout is a particularly acute form of stress that is job related. While burnout as a concept has been applied to everything from jogging to parenting, it is largely a concept that is used for work-related stress. Those experiencing burnout are often in jobs where they have to deal with people on a regular basis. They experience three unique symptoms: (1) emotional exhaustion, wherein they have a loss of energy and a feeling of depletion; (2) depersonalization, in which they have negative or inappropriate attitudes toward those with whom they work; and (3) a lessened sense of personal accomplishment with low morale and reduced productivity or capability. The job environment and the personality of the burned-out person are contributing factors to burnout. Exploring alternative ways of thinking about and dealing with the job are helpful starters. If the burnout continues, the help of a professional is often a good alternative.

Post-traumatic stress disorder (PTSD) results from a particular catastrophic event in the life of a person. The stress lies not in the way a person thinks about an event but in the greatness of the traumatic event itself. A person may have experienced a life-threatening or destructive event or may have witnessed other persons experiencing the same. Car accidents, fire, flood, earthquakes, war and physical and sexual assault are examples of such trauma. Persons experiencing PTSD will have intrusive thoughts and feelings, including flashbacks of the event or disturbing dreams about it. They will work hard to avoid reminders of the event and may even numb their feelings generally so as not to feel anything associated with the trauma. They will often have panic responses to reminders of the event (such as a startle reaction to loud noises for someone who experienced the trauma of war) or physical reactions of stomachaches and headaches.

Vietnam war veterans made us most aware of PTSD. As our awareness has increased, we have recognized that persons who were raised in alcoholic families or those who suffered childhood sexual abuse will have flashbacks and intrusive thoughts that are delayed for many years. In the intervening years they develop styles of living in which they have difficulty getting close to anyone; also, they generally numb their feelings and have moments when they feel confused or out of control or "down" that they cannot explain. These feelings will often drive them to talk with others in order to determine what is going on. In the process, memories are often uncovered, and a painful struggle begins to heal the trauma. At other times, a trigger event (a sexual experience with a mate, a particular location, sight or smell) will cause a flashback to a traumatic event and a flood of memories emerges.

Abuse victims often believe that there is something wrong with them and that others are somehow better. They can often feel all right about themselves by becoming dependent on others. Abuse victims have a hard time trusting themselves, others and God. They have a special ability to push others away at the very point when someone might try to help or get close. Abuse victims also have the special ability to distance themselves from their own feelings. They learned this as a means of survival early on, but later in life it causes them problems in relationships.[13]

In our intentional caring, we can be of most help with those who suffer from PTSD by listening, standing with them in their pain and helping them to change their patterns of avoidance. Especially with abuse victims, we should not take offense if we feel pushed away. In addition, we need to be patient if a person does not want to talk or claims to have no feelings, and we must be mindful that trust is built over time. However, often our most helpful response will be in recognizing their symptoms and in guiding them to a professional for help.

8. Caring in a Crisis

Many of the persons who come to us for care will be in a state of crisis. Dr. Gerald Caplan, a renowned community mental health specialist, defines an emotional crisis as "a short period of psychological disequilibrium in a person who confronts a hazardous circumstance that for him constitutes an important problem which he can for the time being neither escape nor solve with his customary problem-solving resources."[1] Unlike the common problems defined in the last chapter, which may reflect longer-term problems in the life of a person or a troublesome style of interacting with many dimensions of life, crises are more transitory in nature.

When individuals appear in crisis, it is usually at a time when they are temporarily overwhelmed. They feel helpless, frustrated and at their wits' end. Normally they would not seek help, nor would they need it. Up to this point in their lives they have had reasonable success with their methods of coping with the world. Now they are faced with a crisis situation, and they see no way out.

A crisis usually begins in a life event that is perceived as threatening. An important point to remember is that the individual interprets the event as threatening. Events that might not be threatening to you or me may be perceived as threatening to someone else. For example, having one's mother move out of town may produce celebration for some persons, but another individual who has depended heavily upon his or her mother for support may see it as a crisis.

When the life event is perceived as threatening, anxiety will begin to rise in the life of the person. If the individual realizes that he or she has the resources to cope with this threat, then the anxiety is diminished. But if the person perceives that the traditional methods of coping are inadequate, then the anxiety continues to rise and a crisis develops.

As we listen for persons who are in crisis we will ask ourselves: (1) Is there a precipitating event? (2) Is there a rapid onset of confused or anxious feelings as the event is perceived as threatening? (3) Does the person perceive that his or her normal methods of coping are inadequate? (4) Is this seen as a more transitory situation, as opposed to a longer-term psychological issue?[2]

A crisis may be maturational or situational in nature. Examples of maturational crises include issues around adolescence, young adulthood, adulthood, late adulthood and old age. Turning thirty years of age, realizing that one is in middle age or experiencing menopause can be examples of maturational crises. Situational crises can include such events as job loss, divorce, assault or rape, drug abuse, suicide and serious financial problems.

Understanding the nature of a crisis and how to intervene with others is quite important. Given the physiological and psychological changes we go through in life, all of us can expect to be taxed to the point of breaking at various points. Whether it be the maturational crisis of middle age or the situational crises of the loss of a loved one or some other unexpected occupational, familial, educational or medical tragedy, we must deal with it effectively or else suffer greatly from it for longer than is really necessary.

For instance, if our failure to get a particular position left us bitter about the opportunities of life, this outlook might endanger our motivation and personal growth at later periods in life. Whereas if we—possibly with the aid of others—were able to come to terms and overcome the sad occurrence, it might be turned into a plus for the future. We might, for instance, be pushed to strive harder at the job we did get, so that getting further advancement would be possible. Times of crises are truly times of danger or opportunity.

The goal of the caregiver in a crisis situation is to become actively involved with such persons so that their resources—and resources in their environments—can be mustered together for action. Focusing our attention on the signs and symptoms of the problem (not the deep-seated causes) and actively discovering their coping resources, it is hoped that the situation can be turned around in a brief span of time. Once this is done, usually the person can learn from the occurrence rather than merely see it as a past disaster from which nothing good has come.

Following the pattern of our intentional conversation that was suggested in chapter 6 **(CREATE),** as a person makes *Contact* with us and they begin to *Reveal* to us the nature of their concern, we will seek to assess (using the criteria listed above) if they are in crisis. If a person is in crisis, as we help them *Elaborate* on the difficulty we will be looking for them to identify the threat as they perceive it. As we look for *Alternatives,* we will focus clearly on resources and the methods that a person has used in the past to cope with life situations.

In crisis intervention, we seek to help the person we are dealing with gain mastery of the situation and of his or her feelings and attitudes as soon as possible. By doing this, the goal is to minimize the harm and show that it was a temporary setback, and that the person is again in control of his or her destiny. This last point is essential if crisis intervention is to work. Not only is it important that we quickly seek to turn the situation around, but the final step is to withdraw once things are on the road to being corrected. To prolong involvement in the person's handling of the problem might result in unnecessary dependence.

Divorce

In some instances, when someone becomes involved in a divorce, the person's employer is called upon to intervene and to help the person get back on his or her feet. With the divorce rate so high now in the United States, this crisis is becoming more and more common. The hardship that divorce causes for the people who are involved is usually quite notable.

The disruption to children, lifestyle and a familiar role within society may distress someone to such an extent that all phases of life, including employment, are affected. This happened to Jane, a successful account executive for an advertising agency. After having worked for the firm for ten months in a key position without any problems, she began coming in late and appeared apathetic on the job. Her boss, Bill, did not say anything because he felt it was a temporary situation that Jane would correct herself. When it went on for well over a week, Bill called Jane in and found out that Jane's husband had sued for divorce. In Bill's assessment, he noted the precipitating event, the rapid onset of the problem perceived as a threat to Jane, the fact that she questioned her own ability to cope and the transitory nature of the immediate problem.

Bill called Jane in for three subsequent talks on the problem. Following the first one, Jane began to feel a bit better. After the final two-hour discussion dealing specifically with the divorce issue, Jane's work improved and she began functioning optimally several weeks later.

What did Bill do? Was it some sort of a miracle? Did he threaten to fire her? How did she improve so quickly? There was no magic involved. He did not threaten her. And although her performance did return quite quickly to its normally high level, it should be noted that she was still upset over the divorce. She was acting efficiently in spite of her current feelings. The reason: she felt more in control of the situation and could see a way out.

The way Bill approached the problem was by following a number of key steps that can be used in any number of crisis situations. Having made contact with Jane, he allowed her to *reveal her feelings openly.* As he helped her to elaborate on the problem, he got her to *define the problem in detail:* that which threatened her and why she felt she could not cope. He next helped to *open up alternatives.* As he tied up their sessions, he *offered active assistance,* showed how her *current success is a prelude to future positive results,* and *reminded her of her value* in his eyes as an employee.

Specifically, Bill handled the crisis situation as follows: *In revealing her feelings openly,* Jane poured out her heart to Bill. He was not pedantic, coarse or disinterested. He heard her out. Following her discourse on her feelings and concerns, he said that she was successful as a mother, friend and employee. He reassured her that this problem was only temporary and that they would meet again tomorrow, if she liked, to further define the problem and plan some specific actions.

In *defining the problem in detail,* Jane reported that she was specifically concerned about (a) her child, because she would need to devote more time to her career since she was now responsible for supporting the family; (b) meeting people socially again as a single person; and (c) handling all home matters as the sole resident parent.

In *opening up alternatives,* Bill suggested a number of ways to handle the child-rearing issue, such as day care, family and friends. Together they looked through the yellow pages and called a number of day-care facilities. As far as the job was concerned, Bill said she could probably switch to full time at the firm. If not, he had connections in the field. Bill affirmed that she would gain more confidence socially and as the sole head of the home once the other points were resolved. He reminded her of her present success in business and in her handling of most of the chores at home.

In *offering active assistance,* Bill helped Jane find a social service agency familiar with divorce issues and got hold of several helpful books on the topic.

In *reinforcing her success* when she started handling the concerns she had, he pointed to her success in doing it as proof that things would work out. He also accepted her right to still feel upset and weak—after all, she had been married for eleven years. He also started pulling back by suggesting she continue to talk to the divorce counselor recommended by the social service agency.

Bill *showed that Jane was still valuable in his eyes* by spending time with her and indicating that he expected her to progress. Seeing that others accept us and believe in us when we are feeling helpless is important to our self-esteem and success in dealing with our problems.

The success Bill had in dealing with Jane was not due solely to his following the logical problem-solving steps above. It was also because he was courageous, generous and balanced in his approach. He did not pull back when she brought up her problem. Instead, he was generous and supportive. He worked with her to deal with the specifics and helped her muster her own personal resources. He also helped her to obtain other supports from the community.

After being initially quite active, he did not continue to be intrusive. He helped her regain her mastery at work and her competence as an independent person. When she needed support, he gave it but he did not maintain a helping role with her personal problems any longer than necessary. He also supported her consulting a professional counselor for other issues around the divorce.

Rather than feeling lost and ineffectual, Jane began to feel renewed strength within several months following the separation. She was actually better off for going through the crisis. She advanced in business, saw males in a realistic light (the anger she had for her husband was balanced by the positive feelings she had for males like her boss) and she socialized well. What could have turned into a disruptive, continuous crisis ending in her losing her job, her stature in the community and her self-esteem, wound up successfully instead.

Suicide

Frustration, anger, depression, conflict, helplessness and despair can sometimes lead to behavior that is physically self-destructive. At one time or another, many of us have thought of "chucking it all," "giving up" or "just ending it all." Others of us may not have entertained such thoughts but have done things that proved to be quite self-injurious in nature.

Although self-injurious behavior is by no means alien to the human scene, both nonprofessionals and mental health personnel alike nevertheless become somewhat unnerved when the possibility of self-injury and suicide come into play. The threat of such behavior can raise feelings of anger, fear, inadequacy or any number of negative emotions in a caregiver. A professional counselor may feel, "If Mr. X commits suicide, it will mean that I have failed; what will people think of me as a counselor? Maybe someone else should handle this case who is better than I." A young corrections officer may worry about the potential of suicide in one of the cells while he is on night duty. He may think,

"What if someone hangs up tonight while I'm on duty? It will be my fault. He will have lost his life because I didn't do something right. They'll blame me." In a similar vein, someone confronted by a friend who is talking about suicide may want to run away from the situation. "Oh, no. Jim is talking about ending it all. I wish he didn't bring it up with me. What am I to do?"

In dealing with threats of self-injury or suicidal behavior, it is important to first *assess the danger of the situation*. Then, it is important to *take appropriate action*, and to *listen and explore alternatives*.

BEHAVIOR CONTINUA FOR ASSESSING SELF-INJURIOUS BEHAVIOR

Thoughts about hurting oneself - - - - - Actual suicide attempt
No warning - - - - - - - - - - - - - - - - - - Numerous warnings

---

Impulsive or accidental - - - - - - - - - - Well planned
Diminished state of consciousness - - - Full Awareness
(under the influence of
alcohol or drugs)
No desire to manipulate others - - - - - Designed to
                                                          manipulate others

---

In *assessing the danger of the situation,* it is sometimes helpful to see self-injurious behavior on a number of continua or ranges of behavior. As shown on the accompanying chart, these behaviors include the actual threat or attempt at injury, the amount of warning given, the amount of planning involved, the physical condition of the person and the motivation for the self-injurious behavior.

Self-injurious behavior can include anything from expressing some thoughts about hurting oneself to an actual suicide attempt. When assessing the severity of a suicide threat, it is important to consider several factors. The chances that a person will act on his or her threat of suicide is *increased* if there has been a previous suicide attempt, if a close relative has attempted or committed suicide, if there is alcohol or drug abuse involved or if the person has a specific suicide plan with the means available to carry it out.

There are other factors to consider in assessing the likelihood that a person will act on his or her threat of suicide. The age and the sex of the person are factors. While women attempt suicide more often, men commit suicide more often. Older men are a greater risk than younger women. If a person is currently depressed, there is a greater risk of suicide. If a person has recently experienced a significant loss (of a loved one, of a marriage, of a job, money or prestige), the risk is increased. If there are no significant relationships in the life of a person, or the significant other is not helpful, there is a greater likelihood that a person will act on a threat of suicide.[3]

Whatever factors are or are not present, it is essential to emphasize that *every threat or warning to commit suicide must be taken seriously!*

One of the prevalent fallacies about suicide is that when a person is really going to commit it, no warning is given. This is false! Some people give plenty of verbal warning ("I've decided to end it all") and also give warning through their actions (they may start giving away all of their personal belongings, for example). Others give no hints. One day they just try it.

In some cases, the tragedy results from an impulsive action or an accident. Some people want to show how bad the situation is but really do not want to kill themselves. This might have been the case with the actress Marilyn Monroe. She probably did not correctly assess the impact of the drugs she had taken and could not do anything to get help in time; the drugs quickly incapacitated her.

On the other hand, some attempts at self-injurious behavior are quite well planned. The person may have plotted in minute detail how and when the attempt will be made. The awareness is there. Fatigue, alcohol, drugs, stress are not present to diminish the person's level of consciousness. The person clearly wants to end it all.

A great deal of variation occurs in the amount of manipulation intended. Some people reach out for help by hurting themselves. From the start, there is no intention of killing themselves; even the wounds inflicted are superficial. Their whole point is to draw attention to their difficulties and force the situation so that someone will help them. On the other hand, others desire merely to end it all. While some in this group feel that death will "show that so-and-so that I meant business," many couldn't care less about the impact their suicides will have. The act is totally self-oriented.

After we assess the threat of suicide, we will want to *take appropriate action.* On rare occasions we may come upon a person with a knife, broken glass or other weapon who is threatening to kill himself. In emergencies such as these, involving panic or a calm deliberation to do personal harm, a number of immediate steps need to be taken.

The first action is a "don't." Namely, don't shy away from the situation. In coming upon a scene that requires immediate action, the worst thing we can do is to shrink from it. We may not do the right thing if we stay, but certainly if we run it probably is not going to help.

When confronting someone who is threatening to jump, stab himself, or do something self-destructive, the immediate goal is to defuse the situation and to get the person talking. By doing this, we can possibly find out why the person is upset and stimulate the individual's will to live.

In showing people that we take their threats and complaints seriously, we give them the respect they deserve. The resultant possible increase in personal dignity may provide just the change in attitude they need to reassume the desire to survive. Also, when we interact in a way that makes contact with them, be it eye contact, voice contact or emotional contact, they may find the support they need to try life again.

While someone stays with them, another should be sent for help. The kinds of supportive persons needed usually include someone they know: a familiar professional figure (e.g., cleric or doctor) and the police. Although we must be as supportive as possible, we must not overstep our authority either. Not sending for additional help or trying to rush a person under extreme stress can result in an unfortunate accident. Remaining calm, trying to talk to the person and sending for help while actively listening to him or her is a balanced, commonsense approach.

Such emergencies are rare. In most cases of threatened self-injury, we are not dealing with people who are in immediate danger. Instead, they are usually at the point of verbally expressing great depression, anger, frustration or alienation, and declaring that suicide may be the only way out.

In such instances, the first rule is to *listen and explore alternatives*. The pattern can be the same as any conversation with a goal as we intentionally listen. This is not the time for pep talks; it is the time to get people to open up and air their feelings. In setting up a situation that is warm and accepting and in which a helper shows that he or she will not become so fearful as to withdraw, people in distress are allowed to take the first steps toward recovery. Where there is hope, there is a chance. And with belief in a chance and the presence of someone to talk to, improvement can become a very realistic possibility to them.

This helpful listening approach is appropriate for someone who is talking about suicide, but is also helpful when someone has come out of the hospital after having attempted suicide. Often we will avoid such persons because we do not know what to say. In fact, we need to be available to such persons and focus on helping them talk about the particular threats that they perceived in their lives.

Whether we are talking with someone who is threatening suicide or dealing with someone who has just returned from the hospital, we can help him or her explore alternatives and actively suggest other resources. Looking at alternative ways of thinking or helping a person focus on how he or she has coped in the past works to overcome feelings of helplessness. Outside resources can also be actively pursued. If the person belongs to an organized religion, encouraging the use of rabbi, priest, minister, brother, sister or other religious figure may be appropriate. Also, a referral to a psychotherapist, local community mental health clinic or a pastoral counseling center is helpful. The goal is to put them in touch with someone who is trained to deal with extreme depression. (In an extreme situation where the person is threatening imminent suicide, the person should be accompanied to the emergency room of the local hospital.) In doing this, though, we should also emphasize that we are still available to listen to them as well.

Sue was relatively new to the area with no significant other in her life. For the first time, she was living in a stressful urban environment and finding that her job was overwhelming. The pressure of work led to a series of mistakes. Being a perfectionist, she could not stop thinking about the mistakes. Instead, she felt guilty. She called her parents for support, taking a risk that they would help her, since the family did not have a history of being emotionally close. When her parents did not take her seriously and changed the subject of the conversation, Sue hung up and took an overdose of pills. The pills did not kill her but made her very sleepy.

When the effect of the pills wore off, she went to work, and from there called her pastor and told him what she had done. She said she was going to try again. Her plan was specific and she had access to more potent medication. The pastor assessed the seriousness of her threat and decided that immediate action was necessary. He got Sue to put another church member on the phone who worked in the same office. The pastor asked the church member to stay with Sue until he could get there. Upon his arrival, the pastor accompanied Sue to the local emergency room. She was admitted to the hospital and stayed for several days. Sue was put on an antidepressant and arrangements were made for follow-up care with a psychiatrist upon her discharge.

Sue's pastor visited her while she was in the hospital. After she came out of the hospital, he was intentional about listening to her story. He helped her to verbalize the significance of her parents' reaction and the loss stemming from the fact that she would never get from them what she wanted. Her perceived threat was that if her parents could not care for her in an appropriate way, then no one would ever be able to care for her. Her pastor helped her remember how others had cared for her in the past and how she could take action to develop similar relationships in her new environment. She worked on deepening her communication with her roommates. In addition, she took specific action to be clear about her boundaries at work: what she could do and what she could not do. Her pastor encouraged her to continue in her counseling and to continue taking her medication as the doctor recommended.

Assault and Rape

Assault and rape are both acts of violence against an individual. In this type of crisis the initial threat is not merely perceived, but is a fact. However, subsequent feelings of anxiety may be due to the psychic injury of the event, with resulting perceived threats to one's personal dignity and future safety.

The physical and emotional shock that accompanies physical assault can be quite overwhelming. Even when a person is accosted and forced to lie down while being searched and robbed, it can be traumatic. The sense of helplessness, the fear of being molested or killed and the shame experience of the victim make assault a situation in which a person often experiences a good deal of stress after it is all over. So although victims may need help for their physical injuries following a physical attack, the brutalization of their psyches must also be taken into account.

Jim is a short, stocky executive in his late twenties. He had worked late one night and was exhausted during his trip home by subway. Upon getting off at his station and starting up the stairs, he was jumped by two young males hidden in an alcove. They put his hands behind his neck, told him not to scream and pushed him to the floor. They then searched him and took his wallet, pants, shirt and shoes. He was left lying on the floor in his underpants, with his hands and feet tied by his socks and some cord.

After Jim got up and found help, he was brought to the police station. Upon giving them the information they requested, he was picked up by his older brother. As a result of the questions that his brother and the police asked, he began to feel a good deal of conflict. On the one hand, he wanted to tell the story over and over again. (By doing this, people can begin to come to terms with a terrible experience and the emotions they felt during and immediately following it.) However, Jim felt shame, impotence and inadequacy as a result of how he "handled the situation." The comments by the police and his brother made him feel more and more foolish, not only because of the way they left him (in his shorts), but also because of the fact that he did not fight back. Both his brother and the police asked repeatedly about whether they had a gun and whether they were bigger than he or not, so Jim began to feel small and cowardly. "Why didn't I do something?" was the question he kept asking himself.

Under the circumstances, neither the police nor Jim's brother had taken the time to listen to the story with the goal of pinpointing the feelings that he had. The threat to Jim's life was only half of the story. The perceived threat to his manhood added to the crisis. Jim needed to talk about the shock, fear and impotence at the time of the attack and afterward. He also needed to know that reacting in a docile way is normal and understandable.

Actively listening to someone relate an emotion-packed incident is one of the most productive intervention techniques we can use. In the case of an assault victim, we will be able to hear the fears, anxieties, anguish, surprise and helplessness that are often there. This is essential to the improvement of the person's state of mind because once the inner feelings and concerns are out in the open, he or she will usually become more manageable. We can then go on to help in alleviating the psychic injury by exploring alternatives for future precautions and safety.

Rape is an act of violence. The victims of the degrading assault go through emotional trials similar to others who have been physically attacked. However, because of societal ignorance and rigid, misplaced double standards, the rape victim often undergoes additional stress.

First, the rape victim should be treated with the same warmth afforded any victim and brought for medical attention immediately. As in the case of an assault victim, we should recognize that the person may be in a state of shock. The individual may seem dazed or show signs of fear. (A victim of rape and assault is frequently threatened if he or she reports the incident.)

The police, hospital personnel, family and friends will have immediate reactions and attitudes toward the rape victim that will affect the victim's outlook. Since many people still erroneously see rape as a sexual act rather than as a violent assault, the people (i.e., the family) who normally provide support for the person may be a hindrance instead. Rather than being supportive, they may inflict onto the victim their own rage, guilt, fear or shame. This is particularly the case when a youth is involved.

On the other hand, people who are educated as to the real nature of rape and who can be supportive without sharing their own misconceptions and negative emotions can have quite a positive impact. Professionals, such as rape counselors, nurses, physicians and social workers, are also in a position to be of significant value in the hospital setting when the rape victim is brought in for examination. However, the bulk of the therapeutic work may take place at home with family and friends.

Whether the person is very demonstrative in his or her emotions, or quiet, calm and seemingly in control, the rape victim will benefit if we take out the time to:

1. Listen actively.

2. Encourage the expression of feelings and thoughts about the attack, even if it seems hard to talk about it at first.

3. Provide an atmosphere in which the person feels at ease crying, screaming or yelling.

4. Be patient with a constant repetition of the events and a continual rehashing of the horror of it: it is usually helpful for a person to go over something again and again until he or she comes to terms with it.

5. Arrange to stay with the person or have some other family member or friend remain with him or her for a day or so.

6. Try to find out how she has dealt with terrible episodes in the past so we can uncover the primary way she can come to terms with the problem. For example, it may be that after some unnerving event, she helped herself bounce back by taking a few days off and visiting her family; this might be a way for her to deal with this emergency.

7. Help provide physical comforts such as a meal, a place to stay and possibly some clothes.

In addition to the above, supporting the person through the hospital process, which is quite necessary, can be of great help, too. If the hospital staff has access to a rape counseling center or a crisis center, and the person seems to want to talk further with someone about it, helping the person to reach the proper contacts is also in order.

If the victim is a child, there are other steps to take. The police and hospital staff are aware of these steps, so make sure the rape is reported to them. Special attention needs to be paid to the family's reactions since they will be taken as cues by the child as to how he or she should feel about the incident. This is the reason that many mental health professionals and rape counselors feel strongly about bringing the family in when working with the victim.

Helen and John were having a quiet evening at home. John remembered that he left his briefcase in the car and, since he was already in his pajamas, he asked Helen to go to the car for him. When Helen went to the car, a man came out of the woods and grabbed her, forcing her to have sex with him in the woods. As he took her clothes and ran, she began screaming. John came running and chased the man but could not catch him. When John ran out of the house, the door shut behind him and locked. Embarrassed, they went to the neighbors for help.

Fortunately, the neighbors were good friends and also good listeners. They listened to Helen and John tell the story in anxious tones and tried not to let their own fears get in the way. This was their neighborhood too, and the thought of a rapist in the area was terrifying. Clothes were supplied to Helen and John. The police were called and soon came. The neighbors listened again as Helen and John told the story to the police. Helen was then taken to the hospital for care and their neighbors came along for support. There and back they listened to the anguish, anger and pain. After they left the hospital they invited Helen and John to sleep at their house. Helen and John felt they would be all right in their own house, but agreed to come by tomorrow to talk further.

The next evening as Helen and John talked through their story again, Helen was stuck on how foolish she had been to go out alone and on the feeling of being dirty and unacceptable to her husband. John was feeling tremendous guilt that he had let his wife go to the car and that he could not catch the rapist. His anger and guilt actually made it difficult for him to be a good listener for

Helen. Both were feeling uneasy about Helen going anywhere alone, especially at night.

The neighbors helped Helen and John explore alternative ways of thinking about the event, for example, helping them keep the blame on the rapist and not on the victim. Helen remembered events in childhood in which she had been attacked by her drunken stepfather. On the one hand, her memories of getting support and working through her fear gave her confidence that she could do it again. On the other hand, old memories were resurrected that proved to be painful.

Because of this, the neighbors recommended that Helen follow up on the suggestion at the hospital that she get counseling from a professional. John also wanted to join her in some of these sessions. The neighbors offered to accompany Helen out to the store, especially at night. They offered her a place to stay when John was away on business trips. They helped John install some new security lights, and they all pushed the idea of a Neighborhood Watch in their community.

After lots of hard work, Helen has been able to go out alone, sometimes even at night. She said that she refused to let the rapist win by keeping her a victim all of her life. Even so, she is wary much of the time.

Drug Abuse

People who are in a crisis over drug abuse will usually present themselves to us in one of two ways. In the first instance, people in a drug abuse crisis may be in an emergency situation and need immediate medical care. As caregivers we will want to be aware of the signs of such an emergency and take immediate action. In the second instance, a crisis may have developed in the life of a person because he or she has been "found out"; that is, an employer or family member has confronted him or her and demanded change. A crisis of decision occurs where the caregiver listens to the precipitating event and the threat involved, and helps the person explore alternatives and resources for change. What follows is a discussion of signs to watch for in dealing with drug abuse emergencies, and an analysis of a case in which the crisis precipitates the demand for change.

Part of the problem in handling drug abuse emergencies is the presence of many unknown factors. For example, drugs tend to mask other symptoms. Multiple drug use makes it difficult to determine the causes of certain reactions. Illegal street drugs vary in their composition and their potency; heroin can be practically "pure" or be mixed with substances ranging from sugar to rat poison. Furthermore, individual responses to equal amounts of drugs under similar conditions can vary dramatically. One person's "high" can be another's overdose; one user's excitement can be another's "bad trip," even though the dosage is the same.

Despite the unknowns involved, being aware of a number of points about certain drugs can help us deal with serious situations and quickly forestall greater problems. If we can act intelligently, we can be helpful and supportive in a difficult situation until medical or psychiatric care is obtained.

We often forget that *alcohol* is a drug. Two things make dealing with alcohol abuse a little easier than dealing with some other kinds of drug abuse. First, since the liquor industry is regulated and licensed by the government, the danger of getting impurities or toxic combinations in a bottle of liquor is almost nonexistent. Secondly, since most of us have had contact with people who have had too much to drink, we have less of a tendency to shy away from a person in trouble with alcohol because of a fear of making a mistake.

However, though alcohol is relatively uncontaminated by unknown substances, often we do not know how much a person has had to drink. This problem is compounded by the tendency of many people today to be abusers of multiple drugs. People now drink and take sleeping pills, stimulants, hallucinogens or other types of drugs at the same time. Furthermore, though we are familiar with alcohol abuse, we may not be aware of some of the more serious complications. These include coma, shock, convulsions, delirium tremens, alcoholic hallucinosis and combative behavior.

An alcohol-induced coma can lead to shock, in which state the person appears pale and sweaty, the skin is clammy, the pulse is weak and fainting may occur. Shock can lead to subsequent total anesthesia of the brain, which is naturally a very serious complication. Anesthesia of the brain could happen several hours after overindulgence in alcohol.

Prior to falling into a coma, the person may appear drowsy, sick and depressed. In trying to deal with a person in this condition, we may meet with combative behavior. The physical complaints reported can include vision problems (e.g., seeing double) and numbness over a large portion of the body. Pallid skin and crossed eyes are other initial symptoms. Later on, a rapid pulse and dilated pupils may appear.

Convulsions are another complication of alcohol abuse. They require medical attention. Convulsions can be serious for a number of reasons. During convulsions, the person may choke from a blocked air passage because he swallowed his tongue, or he may fall and hurt himself. The convulsions may also be a sign of a more serious pathology that requires medical evaluation. Until medical help can be obtained, immediate first aid is required. If possible, persons suffering convulsions should be put on their backs, away from hard furniture, have their clothing loosened and have a soft rolled object (shirt, large handkerchief) put between their teeth so they do not bite their tongue.

Delirium tremens is a rare complication of the hangover stage, usually lasting two to seven days. This condition requires medical assistance because, although there are periods of lucidity, the person is generally not in contact with reality. He may not know where he is or recognize others. Even the most familiar persons may be seen in a confused light. Disturbing, possibly frightening, hallucinations and insomnia may accompany and complicate the exhaustion the person experiences. Besides immediate first aid to prevent injury, hospitalization is required.

Alcoholic hallucinosis is different from delirium tremens in that the person appears fine physically but has periods of hallucination and possible delusions (a systematized false belief—for instance, that someone is trying to kill him). This is a rare condition that can last for variable periods of time, depending upon the person. As one might expect, this complication requires immediate medical assistance.

Combative behavior is another difficulty that we can experience with alcoholics. If the person is not assaultive and one can avoid getting into an argument, combativeness may not increase to the point of needing assistance. However, certain individuals require assistance or police intervention to prevent harm to self and others.

Depressive behavior in the alcohol abuser merits close supervision. People under the influence of alcohol may lose the inhibition that has been keeping them in check, and as a result, their anger may be expressed outwardly (assault, homicide) or inwardly (self-mutilation, suicide). We must pay close attention to the drunken person who becomes so "blue" that self-harm and other highly negative references to self become the theme of his or her comments. Remaining with someone who is going through such a period in this state of diminished consciousness may be sufficient to prevent an impulsive, dangerous action.

Hallucinogens have the power to produce sensory distortions and hallucinations. Included in this group are DMT (dimethyltryptamine), DOM (Dimethoxymethylamphetamine) and the more widely known LSD (lysergic acid diethylamide). These drugs can produce a wide variety of responses. One person may have a pleasurable experience on one occasion and a bad experience at another time. This can be seen in the narrative of a Swiss chemist named Albert Hofmann, who conducted experiments with LSD in the early 1940s. Hofmann describes his first experience of taking LSD as follows:

> Last Friday, April 16, 1943, I was forced to stop my work in the laboratory in the middle of the afternoon and to go home, as I was seized by a peculiar restlessness associated with a sensation of mild dizziness. Having reached home, I lay in a dazed condition with my eyes closed (I experienced daylight as disagreeably bright) [and] there surged upon me an uninterrupted stream of fantastic images of extraordinary plasticity and vividness and accompanied by an intense, kaleidoscopelike play of colors. This condition gradually passed off after about two hours.

He took a subsequent dose several days later. However, his experiences then were quite different:

As far as I remember, the following were the most outstanding symptoms: vertigo, visual disturbances; the faces of those around me appeared as grotesque, colored masks; marked motor unrest; alternating with paresis; an intermittent heavy feeling in the head, limbs, and the entire body, as if they were filled with metal; cramps in the legs, coldness and loss of feeling in the hands; a metallic taste on the tongue; dry, constricted sensation in the throat; feeling of choking; confusion alternating between clear recognition of my condition, in which state I sometimes observed, in the manner of an independent, neutral observer, that I shouted half insanely or babbled incoherent words. Occasionally I felt as if I were out of my body.[4]

When experiences occur that are very undesirable, as in Hofmann's second experiment with LSD, we call it a "bad trip." Medical treatment for this condition usually involves giving medication to reduce anxiety and induce sleep, and having someone provide direct interpersonal support and reassurance while the person is "tripping."

In most instances, though, particularly in the case of a trip that is unpleasant but not so frightening as to produce extreme actions that are dangerous, personal support should be the sole action taken. In such cases, other people should be comforting and supportive and should provide feedback to modify the worrisome experiences. One thing to remember, though, is that the person on a bad trip should not be left alone.

Opiate (e.g., heroin or morphine) overdose is an increasingly common drug abuse emergency. Knowing what to do can be crucial because an overdose can cause vital breathing centers located in the brain stem to be depressed to the point where death can occur.

Intentional suicide by overdosing is more common among addicts than nonaddicts. There are many reasons for this, but two major ones are the overwhelming personal and social problems experienced by the addict and the perception of an "easy way out" by suicide through an overdose.

Accidental overdosing commonly occurs when an inexperienced user takes too high a dose, when the user is misinformed about the potency of the drug (in some cases the drug may be almost pure) or when a user foolishly resumes the same dose after a period of abstinence (e.g., after incarceration or a detoxification period in a hospital). Sometimes, too, a pusher or dealer will decide to eliminate an addict who is becoming a problem by providing him with a lethal dose.

When encountering someone who has overdosed on an opiate, the important thing to do is to call a physician immediately and try to keep the person awake, since depression of the vital breathing centers is a special danger in this case. Some first-aid manuals also suggest trying to induce vomiting.

Problems may occur in the withdrawal stage as well. Barbiturate users, for example, may experience convulsions, psychotic delirium, agitation and other dangerous physical signs during withdrawal. In cases such as these, the person must receive medical assistance immediately.

Cocaine is a white crystalline alkaloid that comes from the leaves of the coca plant. It is a narcotic and local anesthetic known by numerous names such as "coke," "snow," "happy dust," and "white girl." Unlike the opiates, which are "downers," cocaine is an "upper," or a stimulant similar to amphetamines.

Cocaine is the drug of choice for many because it is mythically known as a "risk-free" drug that is nonaddictive. The high that cocaine produces after a few brief "snorts" is often followed by a feeling of being "down," weight loss and, eventually, paranoia, hallucinations and physical collapse. Often the remedy for these feelings is bigger dosages and increased use. Even though cocaine is not considered physically addictive, the psychological addiction to cocaine becomes great.

The use of cocaine does not produce hangovers, lung cancer or marks on one's arm. Initially it seems to produce only positive feelings. But with increased use, a person can become more and more tense and agitated or "strung out." Dental problems, malnutrition, respiratory problems and infections (especially hepatitis B) often follow for chronic users.

As with other drugs, there is a danger of overdose and acute toxicity. There is a special danger for those who are going in for treatment, or to the hospital, to "tank up" so that they can put off the experience of withdrawal. This can often lead to death. If an overdose is suspected, immediate medical attention is necessary and should include close observation of cardiovascular and respiratory functions until help arrives.[5]

A final drug problem that has become quite common is *amphetamine* abuse. Amphetamines, also known as "speed," are used legally for obesity and problems of mild depression. Their illegal use as pep pills is also widespread.

Abusers of amphetamines can suffer from problems ranging from malnutrition to what is referred to as "amphetamine psychosis," in which the person appears to have lost touch with reality, is hallucinating and may be highly suspicious.

A person experiencing amphetamine psychosis may become quite combative and require a place where stimulation is minimal, since stimulation may exacerbate symptoms. Consequently, when someone like this is brought into the hospital, some professionals recommend removing them from the activity of the main area of the emergency room, which is normally quite noisy and active. Our initial efforts to help the amphetamine abuser may include keeping him in a quiet place, but medical help should be secured as soon as possible.

The second type of drug abuse crisis is not so much an emergency, but it is a crisis nevertheless in which a caregiver can play an important role. The following story illustrates this type of crisis, wherein a drug abuser has been confronted with the facts of his drug use and given an ultimatum.

David had used a wide variety of drugs since he was in high school. Marijuana was his drug of choice for many years, but he had also experimented with LSD, speed and heroin. David never felt addicted and always felt in control. He had even had periods of abstinence from drugs, especially when he was focused on getting an advanced degree. But the reality was that he had used drugs consistently for over fifteen years, a fact that he did not like to admit.

His use of cocaine was intermittent at first. He liked the high and saw the drug as "ideal." When his career began to plateau and he felt bored, his use of cocaine increased. He was very "scientific" in his use, knowing how much to use and being very cautious about when he used. But his intake increased.

His crisis occurred when he and his wife decided to buy their first house. His usage was increasing and, unknown to his wife, he had been piling up debts. Instead of paying cash for items, he would take the cash to buy cocaine and charge the item. At other times he withdrew cash from their savings. Within a two month period he had spent $5,000 on cocaine, and his wife discovered it when their credit report came in.

David's ultimatum from his wife was that he get treatment immediately or she would leave the marriage. In a state of panic, David drove to talk to Lee, a long time friend of the family. Lee listened as David vented his emotions of fear and anger. He did not see how his wife could do this to him; it was not fair to force him to decide. Lee listened as David revealed his feelings regarding the double threat: the loss of his wife or the loss of his drugs.

David was not convinced that he was addicted. He kept talking about cocaine as a risk-free drug. He still worked at his job, and he showed no signs of physical problems. Lee asked questions and helped David cut through the denial. They looked at the facts together: loss of a lot of money; nearly daily use over the past two months; loss of weight; loss of interest in almost anything but getting high; increased distance from and fighting with his wife; lying to cover up where he was and what he was doing.

Lee helped David look at the long-term effects of his choices. He clearly did not want to lose his wife. But it was extremely threatening to think of no longer using cocaine and equally threatening to have to reveal to others that he had a drug problem. Lee helped David explore his treatment options. There were several programs in the area. David at first just wanted to attend some Narcotics Anonymous (NA) meetings, but as he looked seriously at the problem he decided to pursue a thirty-day inpatient treatment program. Lee helped him find the numbers to call. He also helped him think about the resources David had at his disposal, including his wife, his own determination, his parents and his faith.

Lee went with David to talk with his wife about his decision. Over the next few days, David balked at his own decision. Lee talked with him a number of times to bring him back to reality and to give encouragement. Lee stayed in touch with David while he was in the treatment program and followed up with David after he was out. David continued his aftercare treatment by attending NA meetings. Twice he lapsed and used again, but he has now been clean for over a year.

Domestic Violence

As caregivers, we may be called upon to listen to the stories of those who are threatened at home and need a safe place. We may also be called upon to take someone to the hospital who has injuries that are the result of spouse abuse, even though the victim may say that the injuries are the result of some "accident." The crisis can be the result of an actual battering experience or the threat of such an experience. The crisis can also occur at the point of having to make a decision to get help or to move to a safe place.

While we can use the words "domestic violence" and "spouse abuse," what we are usually talking about is the abuse of a female partner in an intimate relationship. (Children can also be abused and will be discussed below.) Males are sometimes abused, but it is usually the larger and more powerful male who inflicts the abuse. Records show that women are the victims in family violence 94 to 95 percent of the time and the offenders only 3 to 5 percent of the time.[6] Every eighteen seconds a woman is beaten in this country, adding up to three to four million women each year.[7] Thirty-one percent of all women killed in America are murdered by their husbands, ex-husbands, or boyfriends.[8]

It is no longer acceptable for people to do whatever they want to do behind closed doors. Violence is not an excusable alternative in any relationship. As caregivers, we have to be careful not to collude in the excuses and denial that abound when violence occurs. While people have a right to be angry, they do not have a right to be violent. Because someone is drinking is not an excuse. Because someone is unemployed or having stress in his or her life is not an excuse for violence. Because a wife did something wrong is not an excuse for violence. Because a person promises never to do it again is not a reason to refrain from seeking help. Chances are it will happen again, and we need to appropriately intervene to interrupt the cycle of violence.

There are typically three phases in the cycle of violence. The first phase is the tension-building phase where there is an increase in sarcasm, criticism, anger, blaming, tension and arguing. In this phase there are often cues and triggers that repeatedly touch sensitive issues in each person. The second phase is the explosive or violent phase where there can be physical, verbal and emotional abuse. There can be hair-pulling, pushing and shoving, slapping, hitting, choking and kicking. But there can also be verbal threats, throwing objects, hurting family pets and punching walls and doors. The third phase is the remorse phase (sometimes called the honeymoon phase). In this stage there is remorse and guilt, asking for forgiveness, the offering of gifts, and apologies that it will never happen again. Yet, the cycle continues and returns to the tension-building phase.[9]

Battered women often have grown up with violence, either seeing it (e.g., between parents) or experiencing it firsthand. They come to accept violence as a part of a relationship, or, while swearing that it will never happen in their relationships, end up being attracted to a "Dr. Jekyll and Mr. Hyde," whose violent side is at first hidden. Experiencing shame, often needing protection and support, women become increasingly afraid to resist or speak up.

But we must be cautious about speaking in stereotypical fashion of battered women, and more so, we must refuse to accept the myths about battered women, for example, that they can leave if they want to, or they provoke the violence or it only happens to uneducated women. Most abuse is unprovoked; battering cuts across all class lines; educated women may be at greater risk; emotional and economical dependency on a man make it very hard to leave; and battered women *can* and *do* break the cycle of violence—most often by leaving the man who batters.[10]

Men who batter women are not always violent in other relationships. He can be quite easy-going at work or church. Or maybe the immediate consequences of hitting a boss or friend are too intimidating to allow him to use violence there. Batterers are often very insecure, and it is their female partners that they need as the glue to hold them together emotionally. The male needs to control the female because he fears that she will become independent and that he will lose her. In his attempts to control her and keep her close, he actually drives her away.[11]

Batterers can even be very religious. Rigid roles, hierarchical power structures and means of control can be reinforced by mis-applied portions of scripture. In our roles as caregivers, it is important that we not collude in the use of scripture to keep women in violent situations. For instance, Ephesians 5:21 ff. is often taken out of context to ensure the submission of a woman to any treatment in the home. Such interpreters of Ephesians 5 often start too late and end too early in reading the passage, focusing primarily on Ephesians 5:22 (RSV), "Wives, be subject to your husbands...." But this verse can only be rightly understood by reading on to Ephesians 5:25 (RSV): "Husbands, love your wives, as Christ loved the church and gave himself up for her...," or by backing up to read Ephesians 5:21 (RSV), "Be subject to one another out of reverence for Christ." Truly, Christian marriage is designed to be one of mutual respect, not one-sided domination.

As caregivers, we are called upon to respond to the crisis of immediate violence, but also to the crisis that results from trying to break out of the cycle of violence. When someone comes to us who has just been injured, we need to get him or her immediate medical attention. Bruises on the surface may indicate deeper problems beneath. In insisting on medical attention, we will also need to confront the denial that something serious has hap-pened or that this was just an unusual accident. As we invite people to tell us more and sometimes notice the inconsistencies in their stories, we can mirror back to them the truth of what has happened and often uncover the real threat: namely, that some-thing must change.

Others may come to us after they have been to the hospital, or after there has been a threat of violence or when they are in the buildup phase of violence and sensing tension on the rise. As we hear them reveal their pain and help them elaborate on the perceived threat, we will want to continuously mirror back to them the reality of the situation and cut through the many excuses that ensure the repetition of the cycle of violence.

As we look for alternatives, we will need to help the person assess the immediate danger and explore resources to establish a safe place. We can provide a safe place to talk, but we may need also to offer temporary housing or help them find the same. We can help the person to identify his or her internal resources, which may include a strong faith, skills in coping with past problems, the proven ability to earn a living and the fact that he or she is already running the house anyway. We can help the person explore external resources: friends, family, church, shelters and counseling services. Both the one battered and the one doing the battering need to find group and individual counseling to attend. Compliance on getting this kind of help usually needs to precede marital work and any attempts to return to normalcy in the relationship.

Evelyn was raised in a family where there was violence. She saw her mother and father throw things and saw her father beat her mother. Her parents eventually divorced but still had battles around the children even after the divorce; ultimately her father was killed by her mother while Evelyn watched. Evelyn had also experienced violence; she was beaten on several occasions, but she discounted these experiences as, "I guess I had it coming to me." She was also sexually abused by a cousin between the ages of seven and ten.

Evelyn swore that she would never take abuse in any of her relationships. She had a number of short-term relationships in which she was used sexually, but she felt that she was in control and would always "dump them." This was the case with the father of her first child. She chose not to marry but did choose to keep the child.

When she met Joe, she saw him as different. After six years of dating, they married, and she saw the marriage as a safe place from all the pain that she had experienced in life. Joe was a hard worker and accepted her child as his own. He was an active member at church and respected in the community. They eventually had another child together. Evelyn stayed home to raise the children, and the family was financially dependent on Joe's income.

Communication was never great. Evelyn had learned early in life to be silent rather than share her deepest emotions. Joe had learned the same thing. Often tension would build in the relationship when there was stress at Joe's work, when he felt she was not doing enough around the house, when his emotional needs were not being met or when they disagreed about how to spend their limited income.

When Evelyn came to her deacon at church, she still had a black eye. She had been to the hospital the day before after a fight with Joe in which he ended up on top of her, punching her in the face. She was still in shock. As she revealed her story and her deacon helped her to elaborate, she told how she never thought this would happen in her relationship and how her safe place in the world had been violated. She had always said that no man would ever hit her, and if he did she would be gone. But even in the shock she could not bring herself to think about leaving. She rationalized that this was only once, that Joe was such a good man, and that she knew she could not make it on her own.

Evelyn's deacon helped her talk through her pain. As she talked, it came out that this was the worst incidence of violence, but it was not the first. Joe had pushed her before, had thrown things and had punched a hole in the wall. She had always discounted these events rather than see them as violence.

The real threat now for Evelyn was in deciding what to do. She did not feel safe at home, yet she had nowhere to go. Her deacon explored options of where to go. Evelyn did not feel comfortable with her family and she did not want a shelter, but she did decide she could ask a friend if she could stay at her home for a couple of days.

While they were separated, Evelyn came again to talk to the deacon. They found a support group for Evelyn to attend where she began to learn about the cycle of violence and what violence in the home really was. They also began to explore whether she should move back home with Joe, and what needed to happen before she could feel safe again. She decided that it would help if

Joe went to a batterers' group for men and sought counseling with her.

Joe also came in to talk with the deacon. He was ashamed and remorseful and said that he would do anything to get Evelyn back. He agreed to go to the men's group with some reluctance. He did not see himself as a batterer and did not want to be labeled as such. He agreed also to seek marriage counseling but did not want individual work.

Evelyn began to feel safer and decided to move back home with Joe. She continued to go to her women's group, and Joe did go to some marriage counseling sessions. However, he refused to go to his men's group and would not accept total responsibility for the battering incident, saying instead that Evelyn provoked him. He eventually dropped out of the marriage counseling. The immediate crisis was over. On the surface things looked normal in the relationship, but Evelyn could not trust Joe. He saw her as rejecting him, and the tension began to build again.

Several months later, in the middle of an argument, Joe again pushed Evelyn, knocking her to the floor and bruising a rib on her right side. This time, with the support of her church and her women's support group, she found the courage to leave. She battled feelings of guilt about not keeping the marriage together and worried about biblical injunctions against divorce. She was willing to try again if only Joe would do the work he promised to do. Joe continued to refuse help. He did not feel that he had a problem. Evelyn, after a stay with friends, found her own apartment and a job that enabled her to get by. She eventually divorced Joe.

Child Abuse

In our capacity as caregivers, we may encounter someone in crisis over child abuse in any one of several ways. A child may reveal to us directly or indirectly that he or she has been abused. We may observe unusual signs in a child that cause us to suspect child abuse. A parent may come to us out of concern for his or her lack of control when he or she gets angry. A parent may come to us in crisis because someone has just reported him or her for abusing a child. An adult may come to us in crisis because something has triggered a long-repressed memory of child abuse.

In 1974 the U.S. Congress defined child abuse as follows:

> Child abuse and neglect means the physical and mental injury, sexual abuse, negligent treatment or maltreatment of the child under the age of eighteen by a person who is responsible for the child's welfare under circumstances which indicate that the child's health or welfare is harmed or threatened thereby.[12]

Child abuse can include physical abuse, sexual abuse, emotional abuse, physical neglect, emotional neglect and educational neglect.[13] Child sexual abuse is a particularly prevalent form of abuse that has been defined as any form of sexual contact between a child and another person who has some sort of authority over the child. In child sexual abuse, as in other forms of abuse, the child is in a position of lesser power and subjected to inappropriate behavior by someone older. Physical abuse usually results in injury to the child's health and welfare, and often results in unexplained bruises, welts, burns, fractures, lacerations or abrasions. Physical neglect is the failure to give to the child adequate food, clothing, shelter, education and health care when financially able to do so, and the failure to provide for appropriate care and supervision. Physical neglect may result in repeated hunger, lack of hygiene, inappropriate dress, lack of supervision and abandonment.[14] Emotional or mental abuse is the failure to provide love, affection, a sense of security and the knowledge of limits and consequences to behavior. Often the child is shamed, ridiculed, threatened and forced into unrealistic behavior. It may be observed that such a child has speech disorders and is slow to develop physically.[15]

Sexual abuse involves contact between a child and an older person in authority when the child is being used for the sexual stimulation of that person. Such abuse may involve such things as being touched in sexual areas, being shown sexual movies or forced to listen to sexually explicit talk, being forced to pose for sexual photos, being raped or penetrated with objects, being forced to perform oral sex, being fondled, kissed or inappropriately held, being punished in a sexual manner, being made to watch sexual acts or look at another's sexual parts, being bathed inappropriately, being ridiculed about the sexual parts of one's body, being encouraged into sexual activity, being called sexually derogatory names or being forced into child prostitution or pornography.[16] Children suffering from sexual abuse may have difficulty walking or sitting. They may have torn or stained underclothes and itching, pain or bleeding in the genital and anal areas. Younger children may have inappropriate sexual knowledge for their ages, may withdraw from people of the same sex as the abuser, or may have feelings of terror and rage. Older children may act out sexually, run away, be involved with drugs, have poor academic achievement or have poor peer relationships.[17]

Abused children often come from families that are under a lot of stress and may be socially isolated. The child may be scapegoated, may be forced into the parent role to take the place of an inactive or resistant spouse or may be given special privileges. Abusive parents are often emotionally immature, neurotic or psychotic, mentally deficient or uninformed, criminal/sadistic, harsh disciplinarians or addicts.[18]

While the laws of each state vary, most states require the reporting of even the *suspicion* of child abuse. Professionals who fail to report may be held legally liable. The purpose of laws concerning reporting is for the sole purpose of protecting innocent children. If, as caregivers, we are tempted to ignore the signs of child abuse or collude in pretending that it will go away, we need only place ourselves in the position of the abused child who asked, "Why didn't someone ever notice and help?"

If children come to us with stories of child abuse, we need to listen to them compassionately and without judgment. We need to believe them, since abused children rarely lie about being abused. We need to allow them to elaborate on their stories in privacy so there is no chance of eavesdropping. We need to let them know that they can trust us, and we need to be honest with them about what must happen next.

Whether a child comes to us directly with a story of abuse, we observe the signs of child abuse and become suspicious or an adult comes to us and indicates that he or she has abused a child, we need to report. We may report to a government agency such as Child Protective Services, or we may report to the local police department. When we report, we will want to give the name, address and age of the child, as well as the names and addresses of the parents or guardians. We will want to document and report clearly what we have heard or observed.

Reporting will usually produce a crisis for the family. As caregivers, we may find ourselves in the position of listening to one who has been accused of abuse or maybe even someone that we needed to report. Our task is to try and listen in a nonjudgmental fashion. We need to listen to their emotions (maybe even their anger toward us) and allow them to discuss any threats as they perceive them. Threats may involve not only the threat of loss of family but also threats from other stressors that actually preceded the child abuse. Gently and firmly, we may have to confront the denial of the situation as an attempt on their part to ease the threat of responsibility. Then, we can help them with options for coping and getting help for their problems. They may need legal assistance and certainly will need professional counseling.

Kathy was an active five-year-old who recently started coming to church. While Kathy was new to this church, her parents had attended the church before she was born. They had moved away for a while and now had moved back to the area. They had significant financial problems, and the mother had been hospitalized recently for depression.

Kathy's Sunday school teacher perceived her as bright and energetic on the first day that she was there. She was well-groomed and certainly was not shy. She almost directed the singing and tended to dominate in other activities. On subsequent Sundays, Kathy's teacher observed that she could be very irritable and even hostile at times. She seemed particularly "cozy" with male helpers in the classroom and wanted to spend a lot of time in their laps.

One Sunday, Kathy was playing with the dolls and began directing the dolls in very explicit sexual acts. When asked about the actions of the dolls, Kathy gave very knowledgeable answers about their sexual activities and body parts. Her Sunday school teacher did not want to believe what she was hearing, but she mentioned it to a coworker and asked her to watch for any unusual behavior. In subsequent weeks, the coworker also observed Kathy's doll play. They also noticed a time or two when she had burning sensations during urination, and that her underwear was sometimes torn.

The Sunday school workers reported their observations to the associate pastor, who talked with Kathy during the Sunday school hour that day. She told the associate pastor that sometimes daddy "tickled her between her legs" and that "sometimes it hurt." That afternoon the associate pastor and the Sunday school teacher paid a visit to Kathy's parents and told them that they would have to report their observations to the authorities. The father claimed that he did not know what was going on but that Kathy had spent a lot of time with the neighbors and that maybe they were responsible for this. The father even said that he would call Child Protective Services. Both the father and the Sunday school teacher reported the incident.

Upon investigation, Child Protective Services removed Kathy from the home and charged both the parents with child sexual abuse. The parents did both admit that there were some sexually explicit videos in the house, but both denied any wrongdoing. They were angry at "the system" and angry at the church members who reported them. Kathy's father came in on several occasions to talk to the associate pastor. He questioned how church members could do such a thing to him and threatened to leave the church. The associate pastor listened to his emotional outburst and also confronted him with the facts that were emerging. The father refused to listen, refused legal help, refused counseling and denied that he had done anything wrong.

Kathy was placed in a foster home with one of the church members. Her case went to court and her parents were ultimately convicted. Her father spent time in jail. Her mother was placed in a mental institution for a period of time. Church members eventually adopted Kathy and provided her with a loving environment in which to be raised. She received considerable counseling and suffered from a dissociative identity disorder.

Unlike Kathy, many children who are sexually abused are never discovered and they never tell. In fact, they forget the sexual abuse as a means of survival. As adults they may have vague feelings that something is wrong with them. They have difficulty with intimacy and with trusting themselves, others and God. Their relationships can be characterized by high levels of dependency or characterized by coming close and then pushing away. They may deny most of their feelings and live with a facade of toughness, aloofness, anger or comedy to keep people from coming too close. Others may engage in reckless and dangerous behavior.

In adulthood, the victim's vague, uneasy feelings may become overwhelming and confusing to the point that a crisis occurs, causing the person to seek the advice of a friend or a professional counselor. For others, certain life events may trigger intense, confusing feelings or even those long forgotten memories, and a crisis occurs. Being touched in a certain way, getting married, experiencing sex as an adult, having a child who reaches the same age as they were when they were abused, as well as many other experiences may trigger memories.

In our role as caregivers, we will want to use our usual listening skills, but we will want to develop a few additional goals in listening to the abused person as suggested by Sharon Cheston:

1. Listen patiently, even if the other person does not want to talk. The abused person does not trust easily and has a difficult time exposing the real self.

2. Allow plenty of time to be with the abused person. To leave early may create feelings of rejection or abandonment.

3. Put aside strong feelings and prejudices. Be open and sensitive without being defensive, even if the abused person becomes angry or attacking.

4. Realize your limitations. Always refer the abused person for professional help.[19]

In addition to these goals, it is important in our listening to the abused person that we not suggest events that might have occurred. As we ask questions or help to elaborate on their story, remember that we will want it to be *their* story. We will want to use their words, or summarize their words, rather than asking if this happened or that happened. In their vulnerable state, our suggestions and their memories may get confused.

In the initial crisis it may be hard for the victims of abuse to realize that they will benefit from professional help. In typical fashion, they may belittle themselves for needing help, or deny that it is really that big of a deal. Our gentle insistence will be of great benefit in the long run. We can assure the abused person that we will be with them along the way, and we may need to be intentional about offering our care for the next several months. We will also want to be sensitive to the crisis that the abused person's spouse may experience and the concomitant feelings of shock, rage or helplessness.

9. Caring Enough to Refer

Part of knowing how to help someone is knowing when our efforts will *not* be enough. In standing by another person in distress, there are times when, through our support, active listening, conversation with a goal and assistance in the problem-solving process, we believe that additional help is necessary. We may feel that a referral to a professional is in order, or that someone needs the help of a specialized group or that someone who has more time would be more helpful for this person who needs care.

Once this seems evident, it should be brought to the attention of the one who has come for care and discussed fully. Then, if the person comes to see that seeking additional assistance is best, helping him or her find the appropriate contact may be necessary. Recognizing that one needs additional assistance and that there are many options open when seeking it is difficult for many people to realize. Therefore, a basic knowledge in this area can be most useful for those of us interested in caring for others.

The Caregiver's Own Need to Refer

A vital part of being a caregiver is to know when we are not the right person to care for this individual and to know when we have reached our limitations in helping the person. This is not failure. This is not being unable to help at all. This is learning to deal honestly with *when* and *how much* we can help another individual and learning that often the greatest caring act is to get someone to the help they really need. In being caregivers, we need to think of ourselves as being on a team. No team player is of help if he always holds the ball. We need to see ourselves working with a wider team and being an important part of that team in order to deliver effective care to persons who often come to us first for help.

In assessing our ability to help a person, we need to ask if we have enough time to be an effective giver of care. We may be getting ready to go out of town for a while. We may be overwhelmed at work or with our own family issues. We may be providing care to a number of other persons already. If we try to squeeze people into our schedule, or even give of our time begrudgingly, then we will not be able to meet them on their "sacred territory," and it is best to refer them to someone who can.

There are other ways in which we may determine that we are not the right person to give care to an individual. We may be too close to the individual, too involved with him or her already in another role or too emotional about the issue he or she brings. This may cloud our ability to be an objective listener and resource person. If it is confusing to be in the role of caregiver for this person, or if we already have our minds made up about what they should do before we ever hear them, then it is best to refer. We can also ask ourselves such questions as: Does this person frighten me? Do I feel sexually attracted to this person? Do I feel anger at this person? Do I feel overwhelmed by this person? Do I feel that I am the right match for this person? If these feelings persist we may not be the right individual to give them appropriate care.

Of course, we also need to ask ourselves if we have the expertise to deal with this person's problems. Without downplaying the skills that we do have, it is important to know where we lack skill or specialized training. As suggested in previous chapters, it is important for us to assess clearly what a person's difficulty is and to know when he or she requires professional help.

When we decide that we need to refer a person, we may experience a whole range of emotions. As Sharon Cheston has indicated, we may feel failure, guilt, anger, fear, rejection or grief. The person we are referring may also feel emotions of anger, rejection, betrayal, disappointment, fear, anxiety, depression, relief, anticipation and grief.[1] These are normal feelings and can be worked through by talking to someone else about them and by keeping our focus on what is ultimately best for the person who needs care.

When the Person Seeking Care Needs a Referral

While we must assess our own issues and ability to care for a person, we must also assess clearly when professional help is needed for a particular person and a particular problem. Probably one of the best ways to arrive at a decision is to assess the person's behavior and reported symptoms in terms of the following questions:

How exaggerated or severe is the behavior or problem being experienced?

Is the problem or the symptom very unusual or bizarre in nature?

Is the person quite baffled as to the cause or solution to the problem?

How much is the difficulty interfering with the person's overall functioning?

Does the behavior seem to be getting worse?

What has the person already tried in an effort to deal with the problem?

How severe is the problem? A recent study reported that surgery has often been recommended and conducted when it was unnecessary. In such instances, the trauma to the body and the financial costs incurred could have been avoided. The same can be said of psychotherapy, professional counseling and drug therapy. Psychotherapy and other professional mental health treatments are frequently sought and recommended when their need is simply not indicated. Sometimes people seek it when they shouldn't because of their being misinformed, too dependent or because it is a "chic" thing to do. Some therapists encourage people to enter treatment when they shouldn't because of inexperience, a poor understanding of the limitations and use of therapy or because of plain old greed. Consequently, prior to making a decision to refer a person to a professional, it is wise to look at the problem as well as the other resources available. In doing so the chances are increased that unnecessary cost, time and emotional investment can be avoided.

The severity of the problem is one of the keys to knowing whether professional assistance should be sought. Feeling a bit down, anxious or confused is not cause for alarm in itself. Only when the situation becomes extreme should outside help be considered.

A good example of this is the grief reaction. If someone close dies, a person naturally becomes somewhat depressed. This could last for some time, ranging from weeks to possibly months. As a matter of fact, the person, particularly a spouse of thirty or so years, may have short periods of the blues for the rest of his or her life. This is not cause for undue concern.

However, if the person is severely depressed month after month, begins developing a number of physical ailments, and does not seem to adjust at all, the situation may possibly be abnormal. The key is the *severity* and *duration* of the reported symptoms and observable signs. If a reaction is out of proportion with the cause in terms of magnitude or persistence, then it is usually wise to seek outside help to be on the safe side.

Some examples of types of situations that might point to the need for a professional mental health evaluation include:

Persistent, severe depression;

Overwhelming anxiety;

Frequent loss of self control (e.g., frequent anger verbally or physically demonstrated without the ability to prevent its expression);

Incapacitating guilt;

Extreme hesitancy in dealing with daily problems;

Continuous preoccupation with personal health;

Great irrational fears (phobias);

Persistent marital difficulties;

Spiraling family problems;

Inability to adjust to change;

Excessive drinking, gambling, use of prescribed or illegal drugs;

Chronic sleeping or eating problems;

Inability to develop good interpersonal relations;

Difficulty in holding a job;

Serious school problems;

Extreme dependency reflected in an inordinate fear of independent, adultlike behavior;

Great difficulty in relaxing;

Little ability to concentrate;

Compelling desire to please others—and the fear of not being able to do so.

Are the symptoms bizarre? A professor was once asked by beginning psychology students how one could distinguish between normal and neurotic behavior. While admitting it was very difficult and the line between normal and neurotic was often indistinct, he offered the following basic explanation: So-called normal people get upset, have conflicts and occasionally get anxious. Sometimes when they are anxious or under stress, they use coping mechanisms such as suppression (consciously trying to put something out of one's mind) and unconscious mechanisms such as rationalization (excuse making) so that they will not have to feel the impact of the bad feelings caused by what is happening. Neurotic people, on the other hand, use defense mechanisms to such an *exaggerated* degree that two things happen: (1) people begin to notice that they are strange; and (2) the use of defense mechanisms is so great that it interferes with the execution of their daily activities.

Even given this basic differentiation between "normal" and "neurotic" behavior, there is great difficulty in determining what behavior is actually deviant. What may appear to be bizarre in one culture is quite acceptable in another. What may be unusual for one person is the norm for another.

Yet, a number of behaviors are *generally* termed as unusual and merit follow-up. In most of these cases, the persons themselves question their feelings and behaviors. In the instances when they don't, the caregivers can bring them to their attention to assess their reactions and the explanations given for them.

Some of the more predominant bizarre behaviors or experiences that people most often report are:

Seeing, hearing or smelling things that are not present in reality (hallucinations);

Having systematized false beliefs (delusions), for example, that people are plotting against them, that they have special powers, or that people are watching them or talking about them;

Having strange ideas or thoughts that cannot be controlled by telling oneself they are illogical;

Having unusual urges or compulsions to do things that are recognized to be strange or silly;

Sometimes losing contact with reality and being unable to tell whether something is fantasy or real.

Is the person baffled by the problem's cause or solution? "I just can't figure out what's causing me to feel this way. I've tried everything; I can't seem to get a handle on the situation." Complaints like these are not uncommon because some people are extremely perplexed by the difficulties they face. The problem may not necessarily be a big one, but the cause of it or their efforts to handle it appropriately seem to have reached a dead end. In cases such as these, a friend or associate can often be of help. However, there are other times when no amount of help seems to have significant positive results—then the need for professional mental health techniques arises.

People with pervasive depression and free-floating anxiety that seem not to be associated with a particular cause often require professional help. The problem has undoubtedly developed over a long time, and short-term care by a nonprofessional will probably prove ineffective. Moreover, with regard to a problem that is vague and amorphous, it is easy for a friend or acquaintance to get frustrated and upset in trying to handle it. There is seemingly no end or improvement in sight, and in such instances it is natural to get angry or feel oppressed by the situation.

When the cause seems quite evident but the solution seems elusive, problem-solving efforts with a professional might also be required. Sometimes an educated, warm, accepting family member or friend can help, but there are occasions when such efforts prove fruitless. In these cases, an evaluation by a specialist would be in order.

How much is the problem interfering with daily activities? Some problems seriously affect the person on a daily basis. If the person's anger is such that he or she is losing jobs and friends left and right, then something has to be done. If the person is so nervous all the time that even minimal risk-taking is short-circuited and adulthood is smothered by a constant need to be dependent upon others, then seeking professional support and intervention seems warranted.

Some people respond to difficulties by allowing their worlds to become more and more constricted. Although withdrawing from active interpersonal pursuits may temporarily alleviate the pressure brought on by interacting with others, it is also a nonproductive way out of the anxiety. The more one withdraws, the more one loses the benefits of our social, occupational and personal environments. People are social beings. By withdrawing from social contacts, we are putting ourselves in an abnormal situation.

Another problem in withdrawing from social contacts is that we increase our future vulnerability. The more we are in touch with people, the more we recognize their foibles, shortcomings, beauty and humanness. If we put ourselves in a corner, our ideas become more and more unrealistic regarding others.

Narcotic addicts often blame people in their environments (pushers, addicted friends, unsupportive parents) for their problems. Some get so angry and vindictive that during their initial rehabilitation period they declare their intentions not to "bother with anybody" upon release. In working with them, one of the goals is to show them that it is important to be discriminating in choosing with whom they spend their time. However, cutting themselves off from everyone until they find the one person they can trust may be frustrating and lead to disillusionment because once they get fed up with being alone they might reach out in desperation, be disappointed in an inadequate response and return to the shell.

Withdrawing from an environment that is anxiety-producing can be a Catch-22 situation in the making. The more a person withdraws, the more sensitive he or she becomes to the comments and harmless barbs of others, and this leads to further withdrawal. Some avoidance of our problems is understandable, but when avoidance becomes so pervasive that it interferes with our daily activities, a mental health evaluation is indicated.

Does the behavior seem to be getting worse? With the exception of rare mental health emergencies or crises, most of the problems that debilitate people are quite insidious in nature. They develop by such imperceptible degrees that the upset or anxious individual may not even recognize that the problem has gotten out of hand. In assessing someone who has come for care, therefore, we always look for the baseline. When did the problem start? How bad was it then? What is the impact of it now? Through questions like these, the comparison can be brought into the open so that both the helper and the person needing care can see the status of the difficulty.

If the person has gotten to the point where he or she feels overwhelmed by the problem even after seeking help from friends, relatives and community supports such as the family physician, then further professional help from a mental health specialist would seem warranted.

What has the person already done to deal with the problem? This question refers specifically to whether the person has already tapped other resources in the community to help with the problem. In other words, have they already talked with their physician, religious leader or other significant person who might normally fill an informal family counseling role?

Utilizing these resources is an important step because it may make additional assistance unnecessary. Many members of the clergy have counseling experience and training, and can intervene to short-circuit a problem before it gets worse. Physicians can sometimes provide the reassurance and temporary medication to get a person through a crisis so it does not develop into a prolonged problem. Also, the physician and other influential professionals with whom the person has contact can often recommend a psychologist, social worker, family counselor, pastoral counselor or psychiatrist with whom they have had positive contact. Finding out who the person has already approached is important before talking with them about going to a therapist.

How to Suggest Professional Help

Recognizing that someone appears to need professional help is only the first step. Telling him or her that they may need it can be an ordeal in itself because of the stigma attached to seeking help in the area of emotional or mental health.

Being in therapy can be viewed in either very negative or very desirable terms. Some feel that psychotherapy is very "chic"—particularly if the therapist has the right address, high fees and a known reputation. For a period of time (and still in some circles) being in analysis with certain professionals was the "in" thing.

On the other end of the spectrum, therapy can be viewed as a real stigma. This is especially the case for some families who view therapy as proof that the person cannot "work it out" on his or her own and is therefore considered to be weak. They don't realize that the reason a person may be in therapy is to further actualize certain capabilities and strengths which may be temporarily stymied, and that it takes real courage and strength to get help for one's problems.

The family may also object because they see the need for therapy as a proof of their own failure. Instead of encouraging a troubled or upset son or daughter to seek outside support, they fight it because they believe that if the child goes, it will mean they were failures as parents.

Some people feel that going to a professional for mental or emotional problems represents a lack of faith; if they only had more faith or the right kind of faith they would not need to talk with someone about their problems. Often the standard for faith in the case of emotional problems is different than the one a person holds for physical problems. If they developed a throat infection, they would not hesitate to go to a doctor or to take medication. They also often overlook the fact that it actually takes a stronger faith to gather the courage to seek professional help than it does to do nothing about one's problems.

Dealing with the blocks a person might have against going into therapy is usually necessary when bringing up the topic with someone. There is no way to get around these potential difficulties and no need to try.

Some things to keep in mind when recommending outside help for someone are:

1. Be clear and direct about why you think they should consider asking an expert about the problems they are facing.

2. Be clear in your mind about what you want to say before bringing the topic up. Have your own feelings about therapy clear in your mind, too, and be aware, *prior* to bringing up the topic, of the potential responses you may receive. This will reduce the chance that you will seem self-conscious about discussing it and the chance that the other person will feel uncomfortable as a result of your own uneasiness.

3. Bring up the topic in a private area. This is a serious and personal issue, and it should be given the privacy and attention it deserves. If the person responds by joking, do not jump in and fool around as well. Some people laugh when they are nervous. You do not want to convey the feeling that you think the problem of emotional distress is a funny or unusual one.

4. If confronted with resistance regarding going to a "shrink," the role of a clinical social worker, psychiatrist, pastoral counselor or psychologist should be viewed from the perspective of a specialist in interpersonal relations and mental health. They probably would not hesitate to go to a medical specialist or lawyer, so why should they balk at going to another type of specialist who can possibly facilitate their handling of life's issues? One definition of therapy is that it is an intensified form of the normal process of growth.

5. Reading can be encouraged on the topic. There are a number of books published on this subject that can be quite helpful. Perusing the shelves of the local library or bookstore will often produce a book that speaks directly to a person's need.

In conducting the discussion in the above manner, while leaving ample room for the person to react and ask questions, the topic of therapy can usually be broached in a very beneficial fashion, with a minimum amount of discomfort for both the caregiver and the person needing care.

When discussing obtaining professional assistance, it is

very important to help the person develop a proper consumer's attitude. Mental health therapies such as psychotherapy, drug therapy and behavior therapy represent a service, not a magical ceremony. The more a person knows about the services available and what they entail, the better off he or she will be.

In trying to inform the person of the nature of therapy, we should try to provide at least some information in the following areas:

What to expect when going for a mental health evaluation;
What settings one can go to for help;
The different professions offering mental health assistance and how to find a therapist;
The major types of therapies;
The general fee range, possible insurance reimbursement and commitment expected when in therapy;
The rights one has as a person in therapy.

Given the broad range of issues the person may be concerned about in going for help, other questions and areas may be touched upon. However, the topics listed above will deal with most of the questions people present.

The Mental Health Evaluation

What should be expected when going for a mental health evaluation? The particular style of the evaluation may differ from setting to setting and therapist to therapist, but there are a number of common characteristics that can be described. For example, most professionals will spend one to three sessions eliciting information. Some may also employ psychological testing if the interviews do not seem to provide them with enough data to make an initial assessment. By the end of the evaluation period, enough information should be out in the open for feedback to be given to the person as to what kind of treatment, if any, is needed. If professional assistance is required and the person wishes to enter counseling or some type of therapy, then the ground rules should be set. Essentially, such information is given along with an agreement on the therapeutic goals.

Deciding on therapeutic goals is quite essential since it will provide the framework for subsequent sessions. These goals will usually be set according to the person's responses to the following questions:

What problem brings you in?
How long has this difficulty been bothering you?
What made you come in now for treatment?
How have you tried to handle this difficulty in the past?
What do you think is causing it?
What kinds of problems has this difficulty been causing you in life?
Are there times when the problem seems to be worse?
What do you think professional treatment can do for you?
What are some other, possibly related, issues you want to work on?
What are the assets and limitations you feel you have in dealing with these problems?

In an evaluation, then, the person is expected to provide details about the complaint, what has been done about it, how it is impacting the person's overall functioning, and what the person's expectations are for professional treatment. Based on the answers to these questions, and possibly on some information about the person's past and present interpersonal environment, the professional will give her or his opinion about treatment. With this opinion out in the open, goals can be formulated and the ground rules of therapy set out clearly so that each participant knows his or her responsibilities.

Ground Rules of Therapy

Before making a verbal contract to enter into any treatment, the following information should be obtained by the client or patient:

When will the treatment begin?
How long will each session last?
What will the cost be for each session?

What will the arrangements be for payment?
What if a session has to be missed?
What will the person be expected to do in treatment?
How long will the treatment go on?

Finding out when treatment can begin is important because many clinics and practitioners are quite backlogged with an ongoing caseload. Consequently, though the intake evaluation may be done almost immediately after calling for an appointment, treatment may be postponed for weeks or months.

Sessions usually last between thirty minutes and an hour and can occur from one to five times per week. On the average, unless the treatment of choice is psychoanalysis, the person usually is asked to come in one or two times per week for sessions.

The cost for therapy or professional counseling varies a good deal, depending on whether the treatment is done in a clinic or through a private office or agency. The fee range in clinics is $10 to $30. Private treatment is considerably higher: $50 to $125 per session with an initial evaluation session usually being higher. The average cost per treatment also varies according to geography and is naturally subject to change. Some pastoral counseling centers and other providers have scholarships created through donations that enable them to adjust payment according to a person's income.

The arrangements for payment should also be discussed. Some therapists require payment after every session while others will permit the patient to pay at the end of the month. The client's insurance is also a factor. Most private therapists require payment for services and leave it to the patient to get reimbursement, if possible, from his or her health insurance company. Most clinics, and a minority of therapists, however, are willing to take part of the fee and wait to be reimbursed by the insurance company. This arrangement is more frequently made when the patient is having problems meeting the medical bills because of low income. In either situation, it is best to discuss insurance issues early. Many therapists will ask for insurance information over the phone prior to the first visit in order to be clear about the nature of payment.

If a session is missed, there is almost always a general rule that twenty-four hours' prior notice must be given or else the patient must pay for the session. One reason for this is that the therapist reserves the patient's time on the same day each week, and filling it on a moment's notice is next to impossible. Another reason is to discourage the patient's canceling whenever he or she does not feel like going. When a person does not feel like going, it is probably one of the best times to go, since such feelings can then be discussed openly with the therapist. In therapy, unlike surgery or dentistry, the relationship with the professional is the most important part of the treatment, not just a secondary factor. It is always best to discuss feelings about the therapy and the therapist in the session, including not wanting to go to therapy on a given day.

What the person will be expected to do in therapy should also be discussed. It will vary from therapy to therapy, but it is imperative that the person be clear as to what his or her role will be and the responsibilities he or she will have. This will avoid uncertainty and unnecessary anxiety.

The length of the treatment is also an important issue. In certain brief problem-solving therapies, the duration of treatment may be only five to ten sessions. However, other therapies will usually require the person to come for a longer period. Though the therapist may not know exactly how long it will take to work through the problems presented, at least by getting an idea of expected duration, the person will not be caught off guard and feel drawn into a long-term situation that was unwanted or unanticipated. Insurance companies today will seldom reimburse for unlimited therapy sessions. Some will reimburse for only ten to twenty sessions. This information also needs to be factored into the equation of treatment length.

Types of Mental Health Workers

"Where should I go for help?" is the next question usually asked by people once they decide to reach out for professional help. The choices in most areas, particularly urban ones, are usually wide. Most areas today have community mental health centers. These public clinics, and the private psychiatric/social service agencies, provide help to thousands of people each year. The names of local clinics and agencies can be obtained from your church or synagogue, your physician, a local mental health association, an area medical college or by looking in the yellow and white pages of your phone book. Probably the best way to locate a clinic or therapist is through someone you know in the helping professions (medicine, psychology, psychiatry, social work, religion, law or a fraternal organization).

As caregivers, it is important that we begin to establish a referral network. When people are in need of professional help, they are usually much more receptive to referrals when they have recommendations from us to other caregivers whom we know. The referral is also more likely to work out if we have some idea ahead of time about a therapeutic "match" for this person in terms of location, finances, approach to therapy and faith tradition. Talking with a pastor or other professional will help us build a list of persons and organizations to whom we can refer when the need arises.[2]

When selecting a service, be aware that most clinics today are interdisciplinary, and that clients may receive help from someone specializing in any one of several helping professions. Similarly, when seeking assistance on a private basis, there are a number of types of professions to consider: social work, psychology and psychiatry are prevalent in both private and clinic settings. In addition, there are certified marriage and family therapists, certified pastoral counselors and other specialists with a variety of training.

Social workers in clinical practice generally have both a four-year college degree and a master's degree in social work (M.S.W. or M.S.S.). In addition to academic work in understanding and treating emotional problems, the social worker has received supervised experience in working with people facing serious problems. While some social workers doing therapy have less or more education in the area, certification and licensing for clinical practice by most states come after they have received their master's degrees and given evidence of a number of years of supervised postmaster's work.

A number of registries of qualified health care providers in social work have been published. Also, the Academy of Certified Social Workers offers a certifying examination to those who meet its minimum qualifications; those who pass can put the letters A.C.S.W. after their names.

Pastoral counselors in clinical practice usually have a four-year college degree, a seminary degree or theological equivalency, a master's degree in counseling or a doctorate (D.Min., or Ph.D.) with specialization in counseling. Pastoral counselors in clinical practice have training beyond that required to be a local pastor. They are often certified by the American Association of Pastoral Counselors or similar organizations. Also, they are often certified or licensed as professional counselors by the states in which they practice, depending upon the laws of those states, requiring them to pass examinations, have several years' postgraduate experience, and participate in continuing education each year.

A psychologist usually possesses a doctoral degree (Ph.D., Psy.D., Ed.D.). To be licensed, he or she must also pass an examination and show proof of supervised experience. Not all psychologists are licensed to do clinical work; instead, their primary interests may be research or teaching. Clinical psychologists, however, have had supervised work with people in distress. Like social workers, there is a registry of psychologists who have fulfilled the qualifications of the American Psychological Association for independent clinical practice.

A psychiatrist is a person who holds a medical degree (M.D. or D.O.) and has completed a residency in psychiatry, which is usually three years of study and clinical practice after receiving a medical degree. If they have completed all of the training necessary according to the certification procedures set down by a board in psychiatry and neurology, they are "board eligible." Not all psychiatrists take the boards, but if they do and pass, they are termed "board certified."

Psychologists, psychiatrists, pastoral counselors and social workers can all perform interviewing, counseling, psychotherapy, consultation and evaluation. Psychiatrists, however, are additionally qualified to prescribe medication since they have medical degrees. A psychologist, pastoral counselor or social worker will contact a physician as a consultant if medicine needs to be prescribed.

The psychologist may also be involved in educational and personality testing. The social worker probably has the most training and awareness regarding the use of social agencies and other community resources. The pastoral counselor has the most training and awareness regarding the use of one's faith in the counseling process. All four professionals have people who specialize further in such areas as psychoanalysis (an intensive form of therapy whose primary goal is personality change) and behavior therapy (an approach whose aim is modification of inappropriate, observable behavior).

It should be recognized that a license or a degree does not necessarily make a professional a good therapist. All that these do is certify that the person has passed a number of exams and fulfilled a number of stated qualifications. These qualifications have been set up for the public's protection, however. So although they do not guarantee anything, they reduce the chances that the person will be treated by someone who is unqualified. Accordingly, when someone goes to a practitioner of some type of therapy who is not recognized by an established training body, that person is taking a chance. This is not to say that such people cannot be of help; it is just that there are greater questions as to whether or not they have received enough supervised training.

Types of Treatment

Therapies seem to multiply like rabbits, and there seem to be new twists and approaches on the scene every year. Yet, despite the array of techniques and philosophies presently in use, a majority of therapies seem to fall into one of the following categories: eclectic psychotherapy, behavior therapy, cognitive therapy, family therapy, psychoanalysis and drug therapy.

The eclectic psychotherapist borrows techniques from a number of schools of thought. The main integrating force is the therapist's personality and background. Usually this type of therapy centers around the patients or clients talking a good deal about what they feel and think in any situations that cause them problems. They are encouraged to bring in their fears, concerns, dreams, daydreams, conflicts, anxieties, joys, emotions and thoughts. In essence they are asked to sit back and let the information flow as it comes to mind. The therapist then asks questions, interprets, reflects and helps to clarify current issues under discussion. The focus is on anything the person brings up, but attention is usually given to interpersonal relations, styles of dealing with the world and what is going on interpersonally between the therapist and the patient.

In behavior therapy there is an interest in dealing with the reported symptoms and signs that the person finds disabling. Though the relationship between therapist and client is important, the therapist wants to work with behaviors that are, by definition, observable rather than with problems of an unconscious origin.

Cognitive therapy works with the thoughts a person might be having, and emphasizes awareness of the fact that the way one thinks affects the way one acts and feels. Clients are taught to pay attention to their thinking and, for instance, to catch their repeated negative or distorted thoughts. Once the client is aware of how he or she is thinking, these thoughts can be examined and replaced with more rational thinking. Cognitive therapy and behavior therapy are often combined to produce changes in the life of a person.

Family therapy is a systems approach that looks at the entire emotional system in which one lives. In a systems approach, often the whole family is seen for therapy. It is believed that what happens in one part of the system can affect the emotional health of someone in another part of the system. For instance, a poor relationship between a mother and a father may create tension within the family system that causes a child to have emotional difficulties. To help the child get better, the system needs to change, including the relationship between the mother and the father.

Psychoanalysis is only for those individuals who have good financial resources, a high verbal capability, and are comfortable with abstract thinking. Psychoanalysis, which usually requires a minimum of three sessions per week, is costly in terms of money and time, and its effectiveness, in all but certain cases, is being seriously questioned today. However, in cases where it is designated as the "treatment of choice" and the person can afford the time and money, significant positive results are possible.

Drug therapy involves the use of psychotropic chemical substances that are usually used as an adjunct to talking therapy. Some studies have shown, for instance, that supervised use of an antipsychotic or antidepressant drug combined with a series of talking therapy sessions is more effective than employing either the drug therapy or the talking therapy alone. The important thing to recognize is that, in most cases, drug therapy alone will not alleviate the problem. Drugs are not a magical cure. They are designed to help a person get through an acute crisis or get to a point where he or she can utilize therapy to achieve a more permanent coping style in relation to the problem.

Consumerism

A mental health expert, like any consultant, is paid to deliver a service. If the person you encourage to get help does not believe that he or she is getting it, then the therapist should be confronted with this fact. The negative feelings the person expresses may be simply resistance to treatment, but they may also be a result of legitimate dissatisfaction. So if people in therapy feel they are not being treated correctly, they should say so.

There are a number of options open. First, they should bring their feelings to the therapist's attention and try to work it out. Often this step will get satisfactory results. If time is allotted to address the problem and still nothing seems to improve, then a consultation with another professional might be in order. People who feel therapy is not proceeding appropriately can rightfully request such a consultation, and no respectable therapist would refuse to permit it. As a matter of fact, if they are baffled, they may request it themselves.

The final step that can be taken is termination of treatment with that therapist. This is a last resort and should only be done after carefully examining the situation. It is always helpful to ask the question: What is it about the therapist that bothers me now that did not before? This should lead to a discovery as to whether it is the therapist who has changed and produced a negative response or whether the person is getting close to something that scares him or her but that should be worked through.

In line with good consumerism, the paying customer should not be subjected to any treatment that is not in his or her best interest. The client should not have to deal with: a therapist who is frequently absent or late for sessions; the breaching of the client's right to confidentiality; treatment characterized by sexist or prejudicial overtones because of one's race, color, creed, age, gender or background; or sexual overtures from the therapist.

The fact that a person is a therapist does not give him or her the right to exploit the client. Becoming a client does not mean that one gives up one's rights. Any therapist who does not show respect for an individual, lacks honesty and displays exploitive behavior cannot be worth consulting. It is as simple as that.

10. Caring for the Caregiver

In the last chapter it was suggested that an important part of caring for others is knowing our limitations and being able to recognize the need for referral. Knowing our limitations is actually a complex process that begins in affirming what we *can* do and ends in a clear decision about what we *cannot* do. Often, however, there is a vague area between the "can" and "cannot" where we find ourselves stretching and testing the limits. Sometimes we may try to help too many people, or we may find ourselves spending an extraordinary amount of time and energy with someone to the detriment of our own or our family's lives. Sometimes we may ignore clear signals that it is inappropriate to get involved with this person, or we may assume that we know more than a professional. These are times when we are stretching the limits and are in danger of doing more harm than good.

All caregivers will stretch the limits at some point. Wise caregivers will catch themselves doing this and will seize the moment to look at their mixed motives for being caregivers. The truth is that there is purity and there is pathology in every desire to be a caregiver. Our pure desire may be in our desire to be obedient to God's command to love others, or in our desire to use our spiritual gifts or in genuine empathy and concern for the plight of another human being. Our pathological desire may be in a desire to "fix" others when we cannot "fix" ourselves, or in a desire to be successful at something or to feel better about ourselves because of rescuing someone in need. Or we may simply be repeating the role that we played in our dysfunctional family of origin where we learned to be peacemakers or caretakers as a matter of survival.

Our pathological desires to be caregivers will emerge naturally in the caregiving process so that we might have the opportunity to grow and become more whole. Our pathological desires will emerge most clearly when we have stretched the limits and when we have failed to care for ourselves in the process. Feeling stretched or burned out, feeling angry when a person is not making progress and feeling resentful when our efforts are rejected are clues that it is time to look at our own motivation for being a caregiver. Likewise, when we catch ourselves taking unnecessary risks, colluding in wellness and ignoring the seriousness of a problem because we want success, or neglecting the needs of our family, it is time to take a look at our mixed motives for being caregivers and to learn from the experience.

Dan was a church deacon who could always be counted on to help. He was often the first one there in a time of crisis and seemed to go beyond the call of duty. There was the time, for instance, when an indigent couple came into town and stopped at the church for some help. Dan spent a lot of time and money getting them a place to stay, helping them get their car fixed, providing transportation and talking to them about their problems. He was quite angry when they simply disappeared one day. Dan also provided a lot of care to the older members of the church. He was always ready to listen to their problems, to run errands and to provide transportation. To many in the church, Dan was a saint. It was, therefore, a little surprising to the pastor when Dan's wife scheduled an appointment and said that she was close to divorcing Dan. She told the pastor that Dan was never home, that he would rarely hold a conversation with her and that he was neglecting his responsibilities as a parent. Dan was obviously stretching the limits and as a wise caregiver needed to look seriously at his mixed motives in desiring to care so much in one area of his life and to care so little in another.

The Danger of Caring

Caring can be a dangerous thing. Helping professionals who consistently work with trauma victims often suffer from *secondary stress syndrome,* or what others call *"vicarious traumatization."*[1]

After working with trauma victims, the helping professional might experience feelings of numbness, avoidance patterns, intrusive thoughts and images or have physical reactions. The professional might find himself or herself becoming cynical and suspicious of others' motives, begin to feel vulnerable or helpless, experience a feeling of alienation from others or even feel a general disorientation.

A counselor who has been working with sexual abuse victims may be walking in the mall and see a parent lovingly touch a child, but what flashes in her mind is a scene of a child being inappropriately touched by a parent. A pastor officiates at the funeral of a beautiful teenage girl who was killed by a drunken driver and who was the only child of dedicated Christian parents who thought they could never have children. Afterward he feels numb and listless for days and cannot figure out God's justice in this situation.

In order to survive, we develop basic beliefs or assumptions about ourselves and the world. Most people operate with a belief in their personal invulnerability, with a view of themselves in a positive light, with a belief in a meaningful and orderly world, and with a belief that others are trustworthy.[2] Trauma disrupts these basic assumptions about the world, not only for the trauma victims, but also for those who care to work with them.

In this sense, caring can be a dangerous thing. We may happen upon stories of trauma or experience it firsthand. We may inwardly recoil in disbelief and feel the pain of the victim. Our explanations about how the world is supposed to operate may not work anymore, and we will have to reconsider our explanations and beliefs about the world to include accidents, tragedy and evil. We may even have to reconsider our beliefs about God and how God works in this world. As one person said after hearing a horrible story of childhood sexual abuse, "If God allows this, how can I trust God anymore?"

To isolate ourselves will increase our danger during these times as caregivers. We will need someone with whom we can talk confidentially: a spouse, a friend, a pastor. Our task will be similar to that of the victim herself: to go through an experience of integration and transformation regarding how we think about ourselves and our world.

Caring is dangerous, also, because of the risk of *burnout*, which is technically a type of job-related stress for people who do "people work." Although it might not be our "job," as caregivers we are constantly involved with people and their problems, and can suffer some of the symptoms of burnout.

Burnout usually has three dimensions. The first dimension is that of emotional exhaustion: feeling worn out, loss of energy, debilitation and fatigue. The second dimension of burnout has to do with an inappropriate distancing and negative attitude toward those who need care, accompanied by a loss of idealism, depersonalization and irritability. A third dimension of burnout is a loss of personal accomplishment: a loss of feeling good about what we are doing, a loss of productivity and feelings of capability, low morale and even depression.[3]

Those who care to minister to others are uniquely susceptible to burnout. Commenting on burnout in professional ministry, John Sanford points out nine special difficulties that the ministering person faces in his or her work:

1. The job of the ministering person is never finished.

2. The ministering person cannot always tell if his work is having any results.

3. The work of the ministering person is repetitive.

4. The ministering person is dealing constantly with people's expectations.

5. The ministering person must work with the same people year in and year out.

6. Because he works with people in need, there is a particularly great drain on the energy of the ministering person.

7. The ministering person deals with many people who come to her or the church, not for solid spiritual food, but for "strokes."

8. The ministering person must function a great deal of the time within his "persona" or mask.

9. The ministering person may become exhausted by failure.[4]

While some of these special difficulties relate only to clergy, many are also appropriate to all caregivers who operate within an institution like the church. Research has shown that all such caregivers need to be aware of the environment in which they offer care and of their own unique personality traits in order to prevent burnout.[5] For instance, if we have a personality that is more anxious, self-conscious, impulsive or depressive, we will burn out in dealing with people long before persons with different personality traits. We need to be aware of our own personalities and take precautions in our caregiving. It does not mean that we cannot be caregivers, but that we will have to be cautious about how much caregiving we give at any one time and about how we nurture our own spirits in order to be effective caregivers.

Furthermore, in order not to burn out, we would be wise as caregivers to estimate accurately the situations in which we work. Ed Bratcher comments that most pastors step into a church situation as caregivers with the "deck stacked against them."[6] That is to say, they are unaware of the powerful forces operating within the system of the church that mitigate effective caregiving. Forces of "we've always done it this way" in the church, forces of family patterns and interactions, forces of biology, forces of culture, forces of addiction, forces of habits and traditions, or what the apostle Paul might call the "principalities and powers" are all stronger than we are and will subject us to burnout unless we realize what we are up against, cease to personalize any failures and enter all caregiving situations with moderate expectations.

All caregivers need to ask the question of themselves: "What will I do if there is no success in, or recognition of, what I do as a caregiver?" Obviously none of us can go on forever without some feeling of personal accomplishment. But the question leads us back to looking at our motivation for caregiving, to our intention in caring. Is this selfless caring connected to some sense of a higher purpose? Or, are we in this caregiving business for other reasons? William Willimon suggests that we will burn out in Christian caregiving unless, "…we develop within ourselves and our ministry an autonomous, inner conviction that what we are doing is worthwhile."[7]

This leads to another danger in caregiving: the danger of *inappropriate caregiving*, which increases the potential for our own *crisis or breakdown*. One is initiated into a caregiving role early on in family life, and brings that style of caregiving into adult life. Allen Wheelis argued some years ago that those who choose a profession of caregiving in which they become intimately involved in the inner lives of people and care for their needs are often strongly influenced by a desire to "alleviate inner conflicts" in their own (i.e., the caregivers') lives. He went on to say that the unspoken desire to work on their own problems by helping others would eventually produce crises of professional failure and stagnation if the caregivers were ever to find real healing in their own lives.[8] Inappropriate intentions in our caring and a crisis in our caregiving ministry, then, end up being two sides of the same coin.

Being overly responsible for the care of others and not caring for our own selves are often clues to an impending crisis and the presence of inappropriate intentions. One recent study found that candidates for ministry who had traumatic family histories, including physical or sexual abuse and addiction, tended to be "…'driven by codependent needs' and may have a tendency to use their positions of responsibility in the church to further their own emotional agenda. Their subsequent style of caring is further observed to be characterized by overresponsibility for others and lack of care of self."[9] In such family situations, a person may have been introduced to the role of caregiving because of the emotional needs of the parents: the parents needed to be parented. In this scenario the child finds security by meeting the needs of the parents but learns to deny and neglect his or her own needs. Love and security are found in being needed. Overwork, perfectionism, addiction to achievement and compulsive caretaking often result and eventually produce a crisis in ministry.[10]

Mature caregiving results when we have seriously reflected upon our initiation into caregiving and have seriously considered our intentionality or underlying motivations for care. Without this work, we will "stretch the limits" or "cross boundaries" in our caring. We will put our lives, the lives of families and the lives of those we intend to help at risk. It will be hard for us to truly stand in the "sacred territory" of the other person; instead we will send a message that it is our own "sacred territory" with which we are concerned.

Rollo May[11] suggests that to understand our inner intentions and not to be fooled by the voices that speak within us, we need to do several things. First, we need to be in dialogue with others. We can only know ourselves in dialogue with others where a true relationship exists. To have true dialogue in relationship opens us to what others may see in us long before we can see it in ourselves.

Second, we need a healthy self-criticism and a fundamental humility. We must realize that we are never free from illusions about ourselves. To "know thyself" is to "know that thou art only a man" and to work through our human tendency to play god. Third, we need to ask if our way of acting makes for the expansion of interpersonal meaning in our own lives and in the lives of those for whom we care. Our work in these areas is really the first step in self-care.

Self-Care

Neglecting to care for ourselves, or thinking that we do not need self-care, is often a clue to the pathology in our desire to care. The story comes to mind of a pastor who would never be absent from the pulpit on a Sunday and would never miss a hospital crisis or an important meeting even though there were other staff members serving the church. He would fly back or drive back from vacation if something happened and arranged his vacation schedule so as never to miss a Sunday. This, of course, was touted as the greatest act of self-sacrifice for the sake of the church. Yet, the truth is that it created a great dependency of the church members on the pastor and met some inner need of his rather than some need of the kingdom. The message this sent to his own family is hard to think about.

An important part of self-care that contributes to healthy caregiving is to take a careful look at ourselves and to *seek self-understanding*. The prophet Jeremiah wrote that, "The heart is deceitful above all things, and desperately corrupt; who can understand it?" (Jeremiah 17:9, RSV) We often do not know what lies in our hearts, motivating us to do what we do. We owe it to others and to ourselves to listen to clues about ourselves and our inner intentions. Socrates said that, "The unexamined life is not worth living." It can be further said that living around someone who has not examined his or her life makes life feel as if it is not worth living![12]

For self-understanding we may want to assess our own personality by taking a personality inventory. The Myers-Briggs Type Inventory, the NEO-PI-R, or the MMPI are all personality tests that can tell us something about how we tend to act in the world. Even if our initial response to the tests is "that's not me," we would be wise to stop and consider that it is "me," but I have not wanted to see it.

More simply, we can obtain clues about ourselves in the course of everyday living. Those who are close to us will often give us clues. A spouse or good friend will often see things in us long before we see them in ourselves. These parts of ourselves may produce irritation in the other person, and they may tell us so. If we will listen and not be defensive, we will probably learn things about ourselves that have roots deep in our souls.

We can obtain clues about ourselves from our own dreams. Dreams have a wonderful way of revealing to us the "shadow" side of ourselves: talents not acknowledged, ways of being that are not consciously known, pride that unwittingly motivates or sexuality with which we have not come to grips. The Psalmist wrote, "I bless the Lord who gives me counsel; in the night also my heart instructs me" (Psalms 16:7, RSV). Dreams are a part of the nightly instruction that gives us counsel as caregivers.

We can look to see where our lives are out of balance and ask ourselves what motivates us to do this. We need to check our balance between: stimulation and quiet; reflection and action; work and leisure; self-care and care of others; self-improvement and patience; future aspirations and present positive realities; involvement and detachment.[13]

We may find that our resistance to seeking self-understanding is high. We may fear finding out something negative about ourselves. We may have a sense of shame, or we may fear taking responsibility for this portion of our lives. Yet, it is this kind of inner listening that makes us sensitive caregivers. It gives us some idea of what the person needing care may feel when he or she begins to look at life's problems. It gives us a sense of humility because we know that we have had to take the same journey to emotional and spiritual maturity that this person has to take. Finally, it keeps our own agenda out of the caregiving process and frees us to be totally present to the other person.

Self-care can be as simple as *taking care of our own bodies.* Eating right, getting proper rest, exercising and relaxing the body are ways of nurturing ourselves and making us physically ready to join another person in his crisis or pain. Because these experiences can be emotionally and physically draining, we need to be ready.

Conversely, *not* taking care of our bodies is often a strong clue that something is amiss in our approach to life that can affect our caregiving. For instance, not taking care of our bodies (often because we claim that we do not have time) can be a sign of overcaring, overresponsibility, and overwork by caregivers. We must then ask ourselves, "Whose needs are we trying to meet in our overcaring?" A body that is not nurtured will often give one the strongest signal that her caregiving is out of line. We need to ask, "What is this exhaustion telling me? What is this illness really about?"

If we are not willing to listen to the signals of our own bodies, we may not be willing to listen to other signals that come from the spirit within. We may not even be able to effectively pray. Kenneth Leech says, "Prayer...is an activity of the whole person, and God is in the wholeness. So the *askesis* of the body is vital, and in the preparation for prayer, attention needs to be given to the achievement of physical stillness, the acceptance of the rhythm of eating, sleeping and relaxing which are essential to a balanced spiritual life."[14]

Self-care that avoids the dangers of caring involves treating ourselves to the nourishment of *regular prayer.* William Willimon suggests that many of our models for ministry and caring today are simply atheistic because we leave God out of them. We do the work, we make the kingdom of God happen, we minister and we care. And if we try a little harder, have a little more empathy, have a bit more dedication, see a few more people, maybe the kingdom of God will come in some small way. But, of course, here are the seeds of burnout.[15]

Regular prayer is one way of allowing God to be a part of our caregiving and ensuring that our way of caring is not atheistic. Prayerfully asking God to be a part of our caregiving, to minister to the other person in the name of our Lord, to give us the right words and increase our sensitivity, to be a part of the revelation that can happen in every encounter not only bring a higher power into our caring, but also enable us not to be afraid since we are not alone. We do not need to be afraid to live in the fullness and depth of human existence, nor does the person who comes to us for care need to be afraid. Rabbi Heschel says it this way:

> [A person's] plight is not due to the fear of non-being [or] to the fear of death, but to the fear of living, because all living is branded with unerasable shock at [the] absurdity, cruelty, and callousness experienced in the past. A human being is a being in fear of pain, in fear of being put to shame. The fear of living arises most commonly out of experiences of failure or insult, of having gone astray or having been rebuffed. It is rooted in the encounter with other human beings, in not knowing how to be with other beings, in the inability or refusal to communicate, but above all in the failure to live in complete involvement with what transcends our living.[16]

Prayer puts us in touch with what transcends our living and spiritually nourishes us. It is essential to our self-care and provides the foundation for our ability to care for others. Since regular prayer is so important, its absence during periods of our lives will give us important clues to our own inner struggle or unfinished business. We can say that we do not have time for prayer, but that only raises bigger questions about why we do not want to take the time to pray. Have we succumbed to the cultural blindness created in a rush of activity? Do we not want to look at ourselves? Do we not want to talk to God for some reason?

Maybe something is blocking us from prayer. Kenneth Leech notes that throughout the Bible there are a number of aspects of human sinfulness that are obstacles to prayer: refusal to forgive; angry and quarrelsome thoughts; refusal to be reconciled; distorted sexuality and lust; involvement in the occult and magical rites; disobedience to God's will; refusal to confess one's sins in the community; and greed and avarice.[17] Noting the absence of prayer in our lives will clue us in to deeper issues in our lives, issues that will probably affect our way of giving care.

Our prayers may take many different forms. Verbal prayers of petition, praise and thanksgiving often come naturally as a part of our caring for others. Yet deeper forms of prayer are also important. Varyingly called meditation or contemplation, deeper prayer serves to focus the mind that has been scattered abroad in day-to-day activities. We can focus on a simple phrase from scripture (e.g., Psalms 46:10, "Be still and know that I am God"), or the simple Jesus prayer ("Lord Jesus Christ, have mercy on me"), saying them over and over until our lives are centered and calmed, and we truly remember the saving presence of God. Or we can focus on an image from our religious tradition (e.g., the crucifixion of Jesus) and let our minds free associate as to what happened and what we would have done if we were there.

This deeper prayer puts us in touch with a way of thinking that is beyond our conventional thought. Urban Holmes says, "Psychologically speaking, meditation taps the prayer of the unconscious because it seeks to deautomate the socialized forms of thinking....[This prayer] breaks through the hard crust of the surface memory to the deeper self, which is relatively untouched by the collective representations of our environment."[18] What often emerge are images or symbols that, in their unique way, put us in touch with the transcendent and give us the strength for true living.

Appropriate self-care will also *nurture the symbolic* in our lives. The use of the word "symbol" in this sense comes from the Greek *symbollein*, which has as its root meaning the act of matching up or connecting. The symbol brings together. The symbol can connect our world with the world of another.[19] Religious symbols have the ability to provide a connection for us with an ultimate and transcendent reality.

F. W. Dillistone, quoting Thomas Mann, says, "To live symbolically spells true freedom."[20] He reminds us of the apostle Paul's perspective that we live in the age of a New Covenant based not on a written code, but in the Spirit: "...for the written code kills, but the Spirit gives life" (2 Corinthians 3:6, RSV). And, "...where the Spirit of the Lord is, there is freedom" (2 Corinthians 3:17, RSV). We find our freedom not in the literal, the factual, the written code, but where the Spirit is allowed to play in our imagination and give us new meaning. Our souls are nurtured, and we are protected against the dangers of overcaring when we allow the Spirit to create new images and make new connections in our lives.

Building on the work of Sheldon Kopp, Kenneth Leech states that the spiritual caregiver speaks the language of myth and metaphor, and must have a way of knowing that has an intuitive grasp of situations that is inaccessible to the purely scientific mind.[21] To be a spiritual caregiver is more than learning a few techniques; it necessitates being deeply grounded in the sufferings, pleasures, risks and adventures of the caregiver and the meaning he or she has made of them through the use of symbolic connection.

We can nurture the symbolic in our lives by listening to our own dreams, by listening to music, by listening to poetry and good literature and by experiencing other forms of artistic expression such as painting, sculpture, dance, theater or cinema. We can nurture the symbolic in our lives by appreciating the beauty of nature and discovering the rich metaphors for living that come from streams and mountains; animals and plants in the cycle of life and death; the process of building up and wearing down.

We can nurture the symbolic in our lives by shifting from concern for *chronos* time and attempting to find *kairos* time in our lives. *Chronos* is the New Testament Greek word for time; it depicts intervals of time or the duration of time. Our word "chronometer" is based on this Greek word and means something like a watch or clock that accurately measures time. When Jesus says in John 7:33, "I shall be with you a little longer, and then I go to him who sent me," he is talking about the duration of time. When, however, Paul says in Romans 5:6, "While we

were yet helpless, at the right time Christ died for the ungodly,"
he is talking about *kairos* time.

In *kairos* time, we shift from busyness to events of meaning
that happen in time. In *kairos* time, we become sensitive to the
right moment for action, or see the wonder of events that are
perfectly timed in our lives. With *chronos* time as the focus, for
instance, a meal is only something to get through as fast as we
can, an inconvenient necessity in a busy schedule. With *kairos*
time as the focus, a meal is a communal event where we connect
with other people, with nature that offers gifts of sustenance and
with the Spirit in our midst.

We can nurture the symbolic in our lives through the
liturgy of the church, progressing through the liturgical seasons
of the year and the rich meaning for our lives of Advent, Christmas, Epiphany, Lent, Easter and Pentecost. Sacraments and ordi-
nances such as Baptism and the Eucharist provide meaning that
connect us with a transcendent God who chooses to interact
with us in life.

We can nurture the symbolic in our lives through the regular reading of scripture with its narrative stories, poetry, prophe-
cies and parables. Jesus often sought to make the connection
between God and his hearers by using symbolic language: the
kingdom of heaven is like leaven, or the kingdom of heaven is
like a man who sowed good seed in his field. Jesus would even
use symbolic language for himself to try and convey the meaning of who he was and how he was connected with God: I am the
true vine, I am the good shepherd, I am the bread of life.

As caregivers, we will encounter people who have lost
their symbols and their ability to construct meaning in life. We
will encounter people whose way of interpreting life is distorted by images of violence, trauma and pain. Nurtured in the
symbols and meaning of the faith, we can help them reinterpret
life.[22] Maybe as we sit and listen to someone's pain, a modern
parable will come to our mind that helps us make the connection between her world and our world, or between his world
and the rest of the world. Maybe as we sit and listen we will
notice that her story is like Peter trying to get up enough
courage to get out of the boat and walk on the water toward

Jesus. Maybe it is like Jacob wrestling with God at the River Jabbok, who gets a blessing and a new name, but goes away limping. Maybe his experience is a death and resurrection experience where he now sees only death and cannot see yet that death is necessary for real resurrection to happen. Having been nurtured ourselves by the symbolic, we can help to nurture others with a depth of meaning.

Finally, appropriate self-care will allow for the *development of friendships* in our lives. The greatest friendship that we are to develop is with Christ himself as we listen to his teachings and follow his command to love. "You are my friends if you do what I command you....I have called you friends, for all that I have heard from my Father I have made known to you" (John 15:14–15, RSV). Yet, as Kenneth Leech has pointed out, it is hard to be a friend of God if we are not capable of friendships with people. We need people in order to grow in self-knowledge.[23]

One way to look at this is to ask ourselves the question, "Whom do we allow to tend our wounds?" First, the question reminds us that we, too, have areas of woundedness in our lives and that we are never completely finished with our woundedness while in this life. Second, the question reminds us that it is dangerous to think that we can tend our own wounds without any outside help. Caregivers can mistakenly assume that they can give care but that they do not need anyone else to care for them. This often creates a dangerous situation where our own wounds fester and eventually interfere with our ability to care for others in a healthy way. Whom will we allow to see our pain? Whom will we allow to see our weakness? Whom will we allow to offer constructive criticism?

Another way to look at this is to intentionally seek out friends whom we can trust and who can provide different roles in our lives. We need someone who can be a "prophet" in our lives to remind us of truth, even if facing the truth will bring pain in our lives. We need a "cheerleader" in our lives who will support us, see our gifts, and encourage us. We need an "harasser" who prevents us from taking ourselves too seriously. We need a "spiritual guide" who will help us with our fears and give us a proper perspective on life.[24]

Caring for ourselves as caregivers is a vital part to the art of Christian caregiving. We need to know our limits and to notice when we stretch those limits. We need to nurture ourselves to have the energy and resources to care. Caring for ourselves allows us to be a simple, nonanxious presence in the face of life's trials, our own and those of others, as we come to be grounded in the words of Jesus, "I will not leave you desolate; I will come to you" (John 14:18, RSV).

11. Caring for the Congregation

We have been learning as caregivers to be sensitive to individuals, to listen creatively to problems they directly or indirectly raise, engaging them in an intentional conversation that allows them to reveal the information necessary for us to assess ways to deal with their problems. We have also been learning as caregivers to be sensitive to ourselves, noting our own levels of stress, our own abilities to set limits, and monitoring any tendencies to overfunction. As caregivers we are also challenged to be sensitive to the institution: to the church or congregation. Can we learn to listen to the congregation in such a way that we hear the problems clearly? Can we respond in a fashion that helps rather than exacerbates the problem?

Religion itself can be healthy or unhealthy. Of course Sigmund Freud thought that all religion was pathological, but this overstates the point. Leech says that religion becomes unhealthy when it becomes a means of escape from being human, rather than a means of integration and maturation of the personality.[1] Likewise, congregations can be healthy or unhealthy. Attentive caregivers can learn the difference between healthy and unhealthy congregations and can choose to respond in a helpful way.

The Congregation as a System

In learning to be attentive to the congregation, it is often helpful to think of the congregation as a system. To a certain extent, this is to acknowledge that the congregation is more than the sum of its parts; it is more than the coming together of a certain number of individuals. What the individuals bring to the congregation, what they have experienced outside the congregation as well as the type of experience inside the congregation, the way the individuals work together, the history of the organization—all influence the congregational system and affect the health (or lack of it) of the organization.

Another way of thinking about the congregation as a system is to understand that there is a certain connectedness in the system so that problems in one part may only manifest themselves in another part. For instance, if we were looking at a family system, we might notice that one child in the family is having a number of problems such as fighting in school, falling grades or consistent disobedience. Without denying that the child is responsible for his or her actions, when we look closer at the system we may see that there are severe problems between the husband and wife that put pressure on the system. The child feels it and becomes disturbed, acting out the disturbance in unhealthy, attention-getting ways. If we are to help the child, it is not enough to try and correct the negative behavior. We must also focus on the source of the problem in the system (i.e., the problems between the parents) in order to alleviate the overall negative pressure the child feels.

In the congregational system, the burnout of the ministerial leader, for instance, may have little to do with a faulty personality of the minister but could be the result of an unrelenting power struggle between committees or church "pillars." Similarly, continual conflict on a committee in which the pastor is always involved may have less to do with the committee and more to do with the fact that a pastor has severe marital problems at home or that a priest is having difficulty with his community. The congregational system is affected by the personal lives of the ministerial staff and key lay leaders. It is also affected by the surrounding culture, issues within the denomination, as well as by the internal organizational structure of the congregation and how issues are processed in that congregation.

As the above examples illustrate, when viewed as a system, the presenting problem in a congregation is not always the real problem. Seeing the congregation as a system, we will want to look less at the content of the presenting problem and more at the nature of the relationships between people and how problems are processed in the congregation. We will also want to ask what might have happened recently in the system as a whole when a problem arises. Systems like to stay in balance, and when changes throw the system out of balance, problems can occur anywhere.[2]

Being Attentive to Clues in the Congregational System

When our bodies are not well, they give us clues to our lack of health. A high fever, congestion, pain, redness and swollen areas all indicate that something is wrong in the body. An organization or a congregation also can emit clues to a lack of health. In scripture, Paul's letters to the early churches and church leaders are full of symptoms of unhealthy congregations. For instance, he warned Titus to "...avoid stupid controversies, genealogies, dissensions, and quarrels over the law, for they are unprofitable and futile" (Titus 3:9, RSV).

Using different language, Merry and Brown[3] suggest that organizations can become "neurotic" and display certain "symptoms" that include the following:

1. Feelings of organizational inadequacy.
2. Lack of energy, low motivation.
3. Interpersonal and intergroup conflict.
4. Much individual frustration and unhappiness.
5. Low morale.
6. Negative selection in membership.
7. Disagreement on organizational goals and values.
8. Inability to cope with everyday problems.
9. Inability to plan ahead.
10. Breakdown in communication.
11. Recurring intensifying periods of crisis.
12. Breakdown of leadership.
13. Neglect of physical facilities.

Merry and Brown suggest that neurotic organizations will have "...repetitive patterns of pathologic, seemingly unchangeable organizational behavior, involving a distortion of reality."[4] For instance, the older suburban church that was once located in a choice suburb now finds that the wealthy suburbs have moved further out. Younger families have moved further out to find the "better" schools. The community around the church now has more senior adults and a much more culturally diverse population. The church leadership consists of mostly older, faithful persons who raised their families in this community. Most committee meetings inevitably end up discussing how things used to be and focus on plans to recreate how programs used to be run or how they have always been run. The leadership is convinced that if this could happen the church would once again flourish with young families and lots of children. Little attention is paid to attracting people who actually live in the community now. Several pastors have come and gone, usually after some controversy or the other. The offerings are down, and it is hard to come up with money to renovate an aging building.

Such a congregation would fit the definition of a neurotic organization. The vital signs are not healthy, and there is a good deal of denial about the organizational problems. A perceptive caregiver would notice the signs of organizational decline and would help to break the illusion of its members. Census data from the surrounding community would begin to give some facts. Shifting discussions from "problems with the pastor" to problems with and potentials for our church vision could create health. Listening to concerns about people growing older and ways of life dying could impact the system and free up energy for the organization.

Pastors or priests will often give us clues to the health of a congregational system. John Savage believes that if you listen closely to the sermons of any pastor, you can tell the deeper struggles that a pastor is experiencing.[5] The sermon topics, the illustrations, the stories told will often reveal more than is intended. Some of what is revealed has to do with personal problems. The pastor who told the story of white water rafting with his wife, of the turbulence, of the rocks, and how his wife was thrown out, gave evidence of a turbulent marriage and an impending separation.[6] As was noted above, such turbulence in the pastor's life can create turbulence in the congregational system. Caregivers who notice the turbulence can help to process the real problems and avoid unnecessary conflicts in the system.

Pastors or priests also give evidence by their lives of problems in the congregational life. For instance, caregivers need to listen closely to the lives of priests who are experiencing a high degree of stress, frustration or burnout. Sometimes it is the personality of the priest, but often the priest is exhibiting problems that are the result of unresolved congregational issues. For instance, a congregation that is being "reborn" may have essentially two churches under the same roof. One church is comprised of older members who have been in the community for a long time. They want the primary focus of the priest to be on visiting those who are shut-ins or who are in the hospital. The second church is comprised of younger families who are moving into the community and joining the church. They want the priest to focus on visiting new residents and on counseling couples whose marriages are in trouble. The church has not resolved the differences of the "two churches" under the same roof. There is no clear direction and no job description for the priest. The priest is burning out trying to please both elements in the congregation and will continue to do so until the congregation has a unified sense of direction. A wise caregiver would notice the signs in the priest but should also look for causes in the congregational system.

The stress, frustration or burnout of the ministerial leadership may reflect more subtle, unresolved issues within the congregational system. For instance, acts of betrayal by earlier leadership may never have been acknowledged or processed in the congregation. The core congregational leadership that asks a pastor to leave quietly after embezzlement of funds or sexual misconduct leaves unresolved issues in the congregational system. The next pastor who comes may experience a high degree of conflict and frustration but has no idea of its origin. The problem was left in the system from the previous pastor due to the decision on the part of the congregational leaders not to deal openly with the issue.

"After pastors" are those pastors who follow after a time of betrayal by the ministerial leadership in a congregation. "After pastors" may find that simple issues within a congregation get blown way out of proportion. Fights may erupt regularly and with intensity over routine church matters. "After pastors" will experience confusion, frustration and high levels of stress, having no clue to the real problem in the church. Only later they may find out that the previous pastor was involved sexually with several women in the church, but the bishop decided to move the pastor quietly for fear of upsetting the congregation or getting bad publicity in the community.[7] A wise caregiver will notice the stress in the pastor and look for other issues in the life of the congregation. In this case, the caregiver will need to suggest a process by which the entire congregation can deal openly and productively with the previous pastor's sexual misconduct. The congregation needs healing, and the pastor's stress is often the first clue to this need for healing.

As caregivers, our own lives may give us clues to a lack of health in the congregational system. We may find ourselves to be overly anxious or angry about certain issues within the congregation. We may have a sense of confusion or dis-ease about events that occur or things that are said. We must, of course, first ask ourselves if this is merely our own personal issue. Congregational life will naturally bring our own unfinished business to the surface so that we may have the opportunity to grow spiritually. Issues in committees that drain us, annoyances during worship or problems with a priest or pastor may be pointing us to our own inner work. And as we do our own inner work, that in itself will affect the health of the congregation. Our presence will be different.

We can then use our different presence to be sensitive to messages being sent in the congregational system. We may feel angry, afraid, anxious or annoyed. In those times, we need as caregivers to ask ourselves what is happening in the system? What changes have occurred? Where is this feeling coming from? We can ask questions and see if others have had the same feeling. We can be attentive and listen for more clues. We can open up discussions in committees or with the ministerial staff. If we can act as an interested and caring investigator and not simply react to the emotion that strikes us, we may help to identify problems within the congregational system and help, by our simple caring presence, with the process of healing.

Small Groups and Congregational Care

Much of the life of a congregation is carried on in small groups. The often dreaded committee meeting is a major place where the inner dynamics of the congregation are played out. As caregivers, we can affect the health of the congregation by how we run these meetings (if we are in charge) and how we listen to the stories of those who participate in these meetings.

Clearly run committee meetings, which keep a balance between the task at hand and the interpersonal issues of the group, contribute greatly to the health of a congregation. As caregivers who are in charge of running a meeting, we will want to know something about each participant in the group, to know something about the history of the group, and to have realistic goals for the group. To run an effective meeting that minimizes conflict, we might do the following:[8]

1. Plan and design the meeting well in advance.
2. Notify participants prior to the meeting about time, place and purpose.
3. Develop a clear agenda that lists goals and objectives of the meeting and that prioritizes agenda items by putting the most important items first.
4. Distribute a clear agenda prior to the meeting.
5. Start on time.
6. Summarize the last meeting and state the purpose of this meeting.
7. Ask for additional agenda items.
8. Try to stick to allocated agenda time.
9. During the meeting create a positive atmosphere, encourage everyone to participate, clarify statements, listen and respond to opinions, help others stay on the topic, express feelings openly and honestly, comment on interpersonal issues and observe the group process.
10. Summarize what happened in the meeting, decisions

made, issues raised and unfinished business before the meeting is over.

11. Evaluate the effectiveness of the meeting.

12. Make sure that concise minutes of the meeting are kept and are distributed to each committee member.

Just as we are intentional in our conversations with others as caregivers, we need to be intentional in the planning and carrying out of meetings. Effectively run meetings contribute to the health of a congregation, while poorly run meetings are a tinder box for frustration and conflict.

However, our intentionality in running meetings is not merely an intentionality that has to do with efficiency. Completing the task of the meeting is only one part of contributing to the health of a congregation. Listening to the stories of those in the meeting is another part.

Stories that are shared in a meeting can lead us a long way off of the agenda and may require sensitive leadership to keep the group on task. But sometimes apparently irrelevant stories carry a deeper meaning that may need comment in the meeting or may indicate the need of a follow-up call or visit with the group participant after the meeting.

John Savage teaches that storytelling is a form of self-disclosure and that story listening looks for the deeper meaning of the story for a person's life as we pay attention to the words, the body language and the tone of voice used in telling the story.[9] There are different types of stories he suggests: reinvestment stories, rehearsal stories "I know someone who" stories, anniversary stories and transition stories. There are also different levels the storyteller can use: data back then, feelings back then, feelings now and self-disclosure.

As a caregiver leading a meeting or as a participant in a meeting, we can learn to pay attention to the stories that are told and appropriately use them to add meaning to the meeting. For instance, Joe was a member of the congregation mentioned earlier that was in an older suburb and was growing old as a church in the midst of a changing community. Joe was known for his dry wit, acerbic comments and resistance to any change. In the midst of a discussion on a motion to allow an ethnic congregation to use the church building regularly on a Sunday afternoon, Joe voiced his opposition and then told a story that seemed partially irrelevant to the discussion. He made an obvious analogy, complete with an ethnic slur, as he talked about this church being like his garden except that they were going to intentionally allow weeds into this garden. However, he went on to talk about how his garden was not the same anymore. The trees on one side had gotten so big that he could not grow certain vegetables any longer, and he had thought about giving the whole thing up.

The leader of the group could have followed up on the story at that moment, but it did not strike him until later. He visited Joe the next day and reminded him of the story. "Sounds like this community is kind of like your garden. I am wondering if you are feeling crowded out by those who used to be a minority but are now a majority in this community. Am I right?" This opened up a lengthy conversation with Joe who talked about the loss of neighbors who had for forty years leaned across the fence to talk and who had been church members but were now deceased. He talked about not being able to work like he used to. He talked about no longer feeling a sense of power in the community and about his fears of losing influence in the one remaining safe place for him: namely, his church.

It was not immediate, but Joe eventually lost some of his antagonism, and the church eventually opened its doors to the ethnic church. Really listening to all the levels of a story first shared in a committee meeting was not the entire process but an important part of a process that helped a church grieve the loss of a previous era and choose to minister to the community in which it now found itself. A caregiver attuned to the story of a committee member was of great help not only to the individual member, but also to the congregation as a whole.

Committee meetings are not the only small groups where an attentive caregiver can affect the health of the congregational system. There are Sunday school classes, youth groups, renewal groups, Bible study groups, study course groups and nurture groups, to name but a few. The same principles of story listening can be used in all of these groups, realizing that to help one person process her story in a group affects the whole group and to some degree the whole congregation.

Small groups that are intentionally formed for the purpose of spiritual growth can be especially productive in this regard if there is a caregiver who can direct the focus of the group. Unfortunately, most groups—even Bible study groups—can be cerebral events that rarely touch the inner heart and soul of the participants and do little to affect their lives at an operational level. For instance, it may be interesting to study the various missionary journeys of the apostle Paul, but the mere intellectual knowledge of those journeys will not much affect the daily life of a Christian. Yet, within the record of those missionary journeys is a life of faith and struggle that can directly impact the daily life of a Christian man or woman. And the impact upon that individual Christian will reverberate throughout the entire congregational system.

It does not take too much effort to develop small groups with a different focus. This is already happening in many churches in a variety of denominations. People are actually hungry for something that will feed their spirits. As caregivers, we can be sensitive to this hunger and help foster spiritual growth groups that feed the soul.

Not every group will have the same format or focus on the same theme, but the following are a few suggestions that will help in the formation of small groups that can nurture the soul:

1. Have a designated leader who will intentionally listen at multiple levels to the comments of participants, encourage participation of all participants and keep the discussion focused.

2. Have a designated theme such as the study of a book of the Bible, a theme from the Bible, a contemporary book or a contemporary theme. For example, a meditative Bible study would focus on portions of scripture around which participants might daily journal their thoughts and feelings.

3. Have a clear contract to which all participants are committed. The contract would include dates, times, places of meetings, the purpose of the meetings, the need for confidentiality in and out of the meetings and the limits to the size of the group.

4. Have definite entry and exit points for the group. Groups that run for a definite period of time and are not open to new

members at just any time help to build trust and to deepen the level of sharing. A group may run from September to December or September to May. A group may run for a ten- or twelve-week period. The beginning of the time period and the end of the time period would be natural points for the entry and exit of members.

5. Encourage group accountability and support.

6. Keep the focus on individual growth in response to the text and the interaction of text and life. Since this is not a psychotherapy group, the focus is not primarily on interpersonal issues between group members, even though some interpersonal issues will certainly arise.

7. Designated leaders of groups need an experienced person outside of the group to process the events of the group and to give additional support and guidance to the group leader.

The following is an example of a nurture group covenant to which group members committed (maximum of ten in the group). The statement of purpose for the group was, "To create an open and loving community where disciples are built up to walk by faith, deepening our personal relationship with Jesus Christ and one another." The group met on ten Monday nights from 7:30 to 9:30 p.m. between October 1 and February 4. The group theme was "developing Christian community," and the text was *Life Together* by Deitrich Bonhoeffer. The group commitment was "to attend regularly; to read selected scripture passages daily; to read the assigned book; to pray daily; to be open and to watch over one another." The structure of an evening was (with some flexibility): 40 minutes for discussion of text; 40 minutes for personal sharing; 20 minutes for prayer; 20 minutes for socializing.

While the format of the small group can vary, the intention is the same. As caregivers, we can attend not only to the individuals, but also impact the system that is the congregation.

12. Common Questions about Caregiving

When participating in small group discussions, leading seminars, or giving lectures to members of churches, civic organizations, and college audiences, a number of common questions about caregiving are always asked. A sampling of them appears below. In some instances the material presented is a review of the concepts, techniques and positions discussed in earlier chapters. Other answers contain information that complements, or builds upon, the material presented so far.

What you've said about our being able to help our family, friends and those with whom we work sounds reasonable, and you inspire me to do it. However, I still have a nagging doubt about the whole thing. Can an untrained nontherapist REALLY do something to help others in distress?

It depends upon what you mean by "really do something." The nagging doubt may be tied to a number of things, and one of them is the expectation you have of yourself in working with others. It may be too high and quite unrealistic. As long as you recognize that you're not expected to provide a *cure* for the person in the form of a magical alleviation of symptoms, I think you will gain more confidence in the positive role you can play. Believe me, if a depressed neighbor or a coworker under stress has someone like you to talk to who will be accepting, supportive, willing to listen and interested enough to begin problem-solving with him or her, your presence as a helper can make all the difference.

I must admit I'm a bit afraid of talking to someone who is having a problem. I worry that I'll say the wrong thing, and the person will blow up or get more upset. Is there anything I can do about this feeling?

Recognizing where your hesitation is coming from is probably the biggest step you might take in an effort to deal with it. The fear you have is an irrational one that is shared by all new professional counselors and therapists. The unreasonable thought is: If I say something right, the person will be cured; if I don't, he'll have a nervous breakdown right here in front of me.

This thought is understandable because most people are nervous when they reach out to others who are undergoing emotional upheavals. Yet, it is not precisely *what* you say that makes the most impact but the fact that you're taking the time and making the effort to say something or silently listen to the other person's difficulty. Through your warm, accepting approach you can help someone. Even if you say something very foolish or provocative and the person seems upset over it, the person will probably overlook it considering your generally helpful stance. And if he or she does get upset, then wait it out and deal with it. You're human, entitled to make mistakes, and the person you're dealing with is more resilient than you imagine. Remember that the person in need is better off having a friend who will reach out to him or her and risk saying something that might not be terribly smart or helpful rather than having an acquaintance who for fear of getting into an unpleasant situation, runs away and avoids the responsibility of friendship.

I've read a bit on listening skills, and I've heard the techniques and principles you've expounded on here. The problem is I can't seem to remember them when working with the people I supervise who come to me with difficulties. So, what I finally do is say the heck with it and just be myself.

Listening techniques are not meant to stifle your personal talents and style of dealing with others. They are meant to extend them more effectively. If people keep coming to you for personal support, then you're probably an easy person to talk to.

The point is to try to incorporate those techniques you hear and read about that fit in with your style.

This can be done in a couple of ways. The first is by so-called overlearning. By reading and rereading a basic primer on listening and questioning techniques, you will soon be able to organize the principles in such a way that they will come to mind without too much effort. The second is by looking at the listening and questioning material and trying to see how the material can be applied in a practical way to your own situation and the specific people you deal with.

If you've had, and still have, problems yourself, how can you be of help to someone else?

Having problems does not disqualify someone from being understanding and helpful toward another person experiencing difficulties. As a matter of fact, people who have experienced similar problems can often be of particular help to others undergoing unpleasant occurrences in life. The caregiver does not have to have conquered his own problems. Just sharing with another one's desire to try to work things out can be motivating. We see this in self-help groups like Alcoholics Anonymous. One of the few possible drawbacks may be that if you are experiencing problems yourself, working with someone with a similar or seemingly overwhelming problem may be too much to handle at that time. Some people undergoing certain forms of depression, for example, feel that being with others who are down is too disturbing for them. In this instance, helping another person in a similar situation might best be put off or a referral given, but this is an exception rather than a general rule.

Anytime I think of myself as a caregiver, I think of a friend of mine and I get turned off to helping. He has a B.A. in psychology and is quite obnoxious in the way he interprets everything and analyzes people. I certainly don't want to be like him.

You don't have to be and you shouldn't be like him. A caregiver doesn't try to inflate his or her own ego at the expense of the person in distress. Moreover, reaching out to other people doesn't include lauding over them and using all kinds of unproductive intellectual devices and games. People who do that are usually somewhat immature and defensive themselves. There is a big difference between being a warm listener and being a know-it-all advice giver. I guess a little knowledge can be a dangerous thing for some people, particularly those who think in terms of power and control of others rather than in terms of generosity.

You say that the use of silence is important in listening to others, but I feel foolish being silent when someone has come to me for care. If someone asks me for help, I feel like I'm letting them down or ignoring them if I don't say something.

When people come to you for specific details about some issue, it would be inappropriate to respond by saying nothing. However, people experiencing difficulties often come to pour their hearts out and be heard. Even if they ask a question, it is usually best answered with a question and followed by a period of silence. This is not a ploy to get you out of having to give your opinion, but rather a means to get the person to look more closely at his or her own concerns and feelings. If we speak too quickly, we cut off the person's ability to listen inwardly and deeply. In caregiving, we believe that being a sounding board rather than an advice dispenser is more valuable and appropriate in most instances, even though it can be more difficult.

I've read a bit about nonverbal communication in a couple of popular magazines. It sounds like a lot of baloney to me. I know I couldn't use it, but maybe I should. What do you think?

I think you probably use it already without realizing it. If you compare your commonsense use of nonverbal communication with the extravagant claims and training regimens offered by some authors, it may not seem that way, but you do.

Every time you look at a person's expression, take note of his or her voice rising, or get an awareness that someone seems uptight or relaxed, you are noting and employing nonverbal communication to understand and deal with other people and their behavior. The point to make about nonverbal communication is that the more you know about it and how you use it, the more you can monitor it for your own benefit.

I'd like to help people, but I don't want to be nosey by asking a lot of questions that are none of my business. In caring for people, how do I know how far to go in what I ask?

The general rule is to ask as few questions as possible. And when you ask something, it should be only in reference to what the person is discussing. If he or she brings up the topic, it is open game, though naturally the person may refuse to answer something even though the topic was originally brought up by him or her. Curiosity for curiosity's sake should not be present in a caring relationship—be it professional or otherwise. When a question is asked, it should be because the answer may shed light on the problem at hand. If it can't help in some direct way, then it should not be brought up.

Can I really help my husband, daughter or close friend if the problem relates directly to me?

When you are directly involved, there are many limitations to trying to help someone else. For example, if you are the person at whom your husband is mad, trying to counsel him would probably cause more problems than it would alleviate. He might think you were patronizing or trying to shift the blame. However, using listening and questioning techniques in trying to get to the bottom of the situation may be quite helpful. For instance, active listening and problem-solving may help you find out what the problem is in more detail and how the two of you can work on it more productively.

I try to be of help to friends who seem to be having problems, but they don't listen. They just do the same thing over and over. It's no wonder they have difficulties. This gets me annoyed, and I wonder why I should bother with them.

The problematic styles people use in dealing with the world usually have developed over a number of years, so they are not going to change overnight—even if they say they want to and vow to do so. When people reach out for help, we have to realize this or, as you say, it can be really frustrating.

One of the traits of a good caregiver is patience. In working with others, we must allow for people to do the same thing over and over again, even if it does get them into trouble. If we are able to stick with them, though, and not be tricked into preaching at them to mend their ways, their lives will be better for it. Remember, our goal is not to change them, but to accept them, allow them to be themselves and help them see where they are in life. If they want to change something, they must decide that—not us.

Every time she has a problem, my neighbor gets teary-eyed. She seems like such a baby. I feel like telling her to bite the bullet. A lot of people are in worse situations than she is. Still, I feel sorry for her and would like to be of help. What can I do?

One thing that might help you to work with her is to recognize and accept her style of dealing with stress. Her childlike behavior is a way of facing unpleasant, anxiety-provoking situations, as are hostility, depression, withdrawal, denial and false courage.

If you can view her style in this way, you may in time become more patient with her, and it may be extremely helpful for her. Not only can she have someone to turn to who won't turn her away, but someone who might in time be able to help her see how her style might be adversely affecting other people and situations. However, the important thing is patience, for if she has someone like you to depend on, it may mean all the world to her and give her needed support to progress rather than regress.

In working with people who have problems, I feel like I'm picking on them. They tell me what they've done, and I point out how they messed it up and should change. It leaves me with an uncomfortable feeling, even though as a supervisor I need to help them deal with their limitations.

In listening and questioning, we try to elicit a pattern of the person's assets as well as his or her liabilities. In caregiving, we try to help them emphasize and utilize their talents in more effective ways. So in caring for others we are not just on a pathology/personal faults hunt. We are trying to point to what abilities they have as much as anything. Therefore, if you see caring in this light and this philosophy comes across, you should not only feel better about what you are doing, but your efforts will turn out to be more effective.

My brother will come over to visit and talk about problems on the job. I feel so helpless. He'll start to get into it and then say he's sorry he's bothering me with it; since I don't know the ins and outs of his business, he's probably wasting my time and his. Then he leaves. I find this a problem with many people who come to me as a friend or a family member; I just don't know enough about the specifics to be of help.

To help people you need to get enough details to get an idea of what is involved in the situation with which they are having problems. In the case of your brother, the situation is his job. However, you don't need to know the business inside and out. As a caregiver, you are a consultant to the person and his problems, which are probably interpersonal in nature. The difficulties he's probably having are with *people,* not policies or business systems. They may be part of it, and this part can be quickly explained to you. But most of his difficulties probably concern the people who make the policies and operate the business systems. In this area, you can be of help if he lets you.

Indicate this to him. Show your patience by listening carefully and try to encourage him to continue. He may not go on and explain further for other reasons (he may feel you *will* understand all too well and criticize or chastise him), but he also may surprise you and continue.

What is the difference between giving advice and giving feedback?

Advice is telling people what to do. It is giving information from our vantage point. Feedback is providing our impression of what *they* have been saying verbally and nonverbally to see if they agree with our impressions. What this does is allow people to see someone else's impression of how they feel, think about and have been handling a problem, as well as the alternatives open to them. Feedback is essentially a reflection process. In giving feedback, we are trying to act as a mirror to get them to see better where they stand and the options open to them.

The timing of feedback is also important. People will often give you a small portion of information and ask you what you think. Your aim at this point is to try to elicit more material through open questioning and reflection of their feelings. This is essential because providing feedback is easier and more useful when it is a summary of their answers to questions and their full discussion of alternatives than when it is given with only a little bit of data in hand.

My cousin seems uptight all of the time. How do I determine whether she needs professional help?

You have done it already. If she is uptight *all the time* and has taken steps to correct the situation, then she probably could use at least an evaluation of the problem. In trying to assess whether or not people need professional help, remember some of the questions you should ask: How serious is the problem in terms of duration and degree? Is the problem interfering with her daily functioning to a degree that she and others readily notice it? Has she sought to alleviate the problem through personal reflection, help from friends and normal family supports, for instance, a clergyperson or the family physician?

How useful or harmful are drugs in the treatment of emotional problems?

Drug therapy, as an adjunct to other kinds of therapy, can be particularly helpful when used with temporary problems or with severe or chronic problems that indicate a need for medication. However, many factors affect the usefulness or potential harm of using drugs to treat emotional problems. Difficulty may arise if a general practitioner prescribes a psychotropic drug on a long-term basis without getting a psychological or psychiatric consultation. Another problem may arise if the physician does not take into account the patient's use of other drugs, including alcohol, when prescribing psychotropic drugs. Still another problem may occur when medication is used strictly for control purposes, for example, when a patient in a hospital is given massive doses of a drug to prevent aggressive behavior.

A final point to note is that when drugs are employed on a long-term basis, they are usually used as an adjunct to talking therapy. In some cases where it is believed that there is a biochemical basis to depression, drug therapy is primary, and little if any psychological therapy is provided. However, this approach is used only in certain cases and is considered questionable by some mental health professionals.

If someone needs to be on medication, does he or she have to be in therapy with a psychiatrist?

No. Psychologists and other nonmedical therapists usually have a psychiatrist whom they use as a medical consultant. The psychologist or counselor will send the patient to a psychiatrist for a medical evaluation and for periodic visits as long as he or she is on the medication.

Are mentally ill people dangerous?

A very, very small portion of the people we label as mentally ill are dangerous. Some psychotic individuals may seem dangerous because their behavior is strange to us, but the portion of people who are emotionally disturbed and who are also potentially dangerous is extremely small.

You hear a lot about middle-age crisis. Is it easy for a seemingly confident man in his forties to get thrown into turmoil by a crisis at that age?

As you might expect, it depends upon a number of factors, including the personality of the man, the type of crisis and the supports and resources he can call upon in his family and the extended community. If the combinations are correct, a person whom you might least expect can be really thrown into a helpless position quite easily. For instance, a seemingly confident and successful executive loses his position because of a merger. If his whole identity and self-esteem were attached to the position, and he had been growing apart from his family and friends, he might find it quite difficult to cope.

Isn't going into therapy seen by many as a sign of weakness? I am reluctant to refer someone to therapy because of this.

Yes, and the existence of this feeling in this modern era is surprising. If a person with a Mercedes called in a mechanic to look at his car or someone with a growth on his arm went to a medical specialist, no one would think anything further. It is logical to get a professional consultant when a problem is perplexing and beyond our range of knowledge.

Yet, given the stigma attached to getting mental health assistance and the myth that everyone should naturally be able to handle *every* personal crisis that comes up, some people think that obtaining a mental health consultation is a sign of weakness. Thank goodness this outlook is changing. People are beginning to see therapy as a facilitating process. And they are starting to take note of the fact that very talented people are sometimes involved in therapy when their growth is impeded by some issue that they are having problems resolving.

What prejudices should a person in therapy look out for when starting the process?

Once a therapist is selected, the patient should be alert to any prejudice that might interfere with the treatment. Therapists are people and, like any group of people, there are some who may be biased in one way or another due to such issues as age, sex, race, creed or style of living. If a therapist seems intent on controlling the client and inflicting his or her own philosophy of life on the client, this should be brought out. Likewise, when therapists make comments that show strong leanings that might interfere with treatment (chauvinistic tendencies or a bias against older persons, for example), they should be confronted with this to see if it is in fact the case.

People are always coming to me for help. I enjoy listening to them and being supportive. Is there anything I can do to improve my caring style?

Continue to read books and articles on listening and caring, emotional and spiritual development and the psychology of adjustment. This will help you to better understand yourself, other people and how to help them. Also, reviewing how you handled something after a person has left is very useful. Sometimes doing this with a confidante who will not divulge what you have discussed can be invaluable.

Look for workshops or training programs that can help you build your skills. These are often offered through local churches, pastoral counseling agencies, civic organizations, seminaries or colleges.

If people are coming to you again and again for help at home or at work, you have already taken the most important step in helping others. You have successfully demonstrated that you are willing and able to reach out to others in need—a not-so-small thing in these times of hustle and bustle, isolation and selfishness.

Time is really an issue for me. When I get started caring for others I seem to get swamped. I enjoy helping others, but it seems to get out of balance. What can I do?

Obviously, you have a gift for caring, and that is why people come to you. Feeling good about helping these persons is a motivator to do more, but it can also be a form of seduction that lures you past your limits.

When we have crossed our limits, we will often become tired and burned out. We are afraid that we will hurt someone by telling them we cannot be of help right now, but we fail to realize the potential harm we can cause by giving inappropriate or superficial help when we are beyond our limits.

Our bodies and our emotions will let us know when we have crossed our limits. At that point, learning to say no is important, but also learning to treat ourselves to that which makes us joyous and renews us is important. Regular times of slowing down and listening to our own inner spirit will keep us in balance and prepare us for times of giving care.

You talk about making referrals for individuals whose problems are beyond our level of expertise. Can one also make referrals for organizations such as churches?

Yes, consultants are available who work with organizational problems, whether they be problems with church staff, helping a church work through unresolved grief and acts of betrayal, or doing long-term planning. Often with issues like these it is helpful to have a trained professional who is not a member of the organization come in and give another perspective on the organizational system. Such professional consultants can be recommended by denominational executives or by contacting an organization like the Alban Institute in Washington, D.C.

In leading groups, I often find that one or two people will consistently dominate the meeting, and no one else can get a word in edgewise. What can be done about this?

This can be a difficult problem for groups and can be quite destructive to the group process. If you have the ability to choose the makeup of a group, you can often head off this problem by being careful in the selection and balance of group members. As a group leader, you can also try to shift the balance in the group meeting itself by calling on others to respond, or drawing out the thoughts and feelings of others.

Also, listen for the stories that a talkative person will tell. Often we can pick up on what is happening deep within them and shift the conversation to that deeper level of meaning. Finally, as we build a relationship with the person who dominates in a group, we can approach the individual after the meeting and talk to him or her directly about what is happening in the group and how he or she can be of help in making the group run more effectively.

Notes

CHAPTER 1: INTRODUCTION

1. For example, see Howard Clinebell, *The Mental Health Ministry of the Local Church* (Nashville: Abingdon Press, 1972).

2. For a more complete historical account, see William R. Clebsch and Charles R. Jaekle, *Pastoral Care in Historical Perspective* (Englewood Cliffs, NJ: Prentice Hall, 1964).

3. Robert J. Wicks, "What Makes Pastoral Counseling Pastoral?", *Church* (Fall, 1987), 35–36.

CHAPTER 2: CARING TO LISTEN: OVERCOMING RESISTANCE

1. Dietrich Bonhoeffer, *Life Together* (New York: Harper & Row, 1976), p. 98.

2. Theodor Reik, *Listening With The Third Ear* (New York: Farrar, Straus and Company, 1952), p. 122.

3. C. S. Lewis, *Till We Have Faces* (New York: Harcourt Brace Jovanavich, 1956), p. 294.

4. Blaise Pascal, *Penseés* (New York: E. P. Dutton, 1958), p. 64.

5. Daniel Taylor, *The Myth of Certainty* (Grand Rapids, MI: Zondervan, 1992), p. 94.

CHAPTER 3: CARING TO LISTEN: STANDING ON HOLY GROUND

1. For more on the "nonanxious presence" see Edwin H. Friedman, *Generation to Generation* (New York: Guilford Press, 1985), pp. 208–10.

2. For further active listening insights see Dennis L. Butcher, *Developing the Caring Community* (Washington, DC: The Alban Institute, 1994), pp. 17–20, and Howard W. Stone, *The Caring Church* (Minneapolis: Fortress Press, 1991), pp. 56–57.

3. Ernest L. Schusky, "Quantum Mechanics," in *Academic American Encyclopedia*, vol. 16 (Danbury, CT: Grolier, 1991).

4. Robert Kegan, *The Evolving Self* (Cambridge: Harvard University Press, 1982), p. 17.

5. Text: Sydney Carter, b. 1915; © Galliard Publications. Tune: Shaker Song, Irregular; American Shaker; Harm. by Sydney Carter, b. 1915; © Galliard Publications.

CHAPTER 4: INTENTIONAL CARING: CONVERSATION WITH A GOAL

1. Erik H. Erikson, *Childhood and Society* (New York: W. W. Norton, 1963), pp. 247–74.

2. Robert Kegan, *The Evolving Self* (Cambridge: Harvard University Press, 1982), pp. 113–255.

3. James W. Fowler, *Becoming Christian, Becoming Adult* (San Francisco: Harper & Row, 1984), pp. 52–71.

4. Howard Clinebell, *Basic Types of Pastoral Care and Counseling* (Nashville: Abingdon Press, 1984), pp. 25–45.

5. John A. Sanford, *The Kingdom Within* (New York: Paulist Press, 1970), pp. 44–59 and 80–94.

6. Fritz Kunkel, *Creation Continues* (Mahwah, NJ: Paulist Press, 1987), pp. 68, 79, 169.

7. Rollo May, *Love and Will* (New York: Collins, 1972), p. 228.

8. See Arnold Lazarus, *In the Mind's Eye* (New York: Guilford Press, 1984), p. 89.

9. See Andrew D. Lester, *Hope in Pastoral Care and Counseling* (Louisville: Westminster John Knox Press, 1995).

10. C. Schlauch, "Empathy as the Essence of Pastoral Psychotherapy," *Journal of Pastoral Care* 44 (Spring 1990): pp. 3–17.

11. Robert Kegan, *The Evolving Self,* pp. 20–21.

CHAPTER 5: INTENTIONAL CARING: THE ART OF QUESTIONING AND RESPONDING

1. The work of Aaron Beck has been popularized in David Burns, *Feeling Good* (New York: Penguin, 1980).

CHAPTER 6: STAGES OF A CARING EXCHANGE

1. See David Burns, *Feeling Good* (New York: Penguin, 1980) for a complete discussion of the topic of cognitive distortions and exploring alternative ways of thinking.

2. Howard W. Stone, *Brief Pastoral Counseling* (Minneapolis: Fortress Press, 1994), p. 58. See also Donald Capps, *Reframing: A New Method in Pastoral Care* (Minneapolis: Fortress Press, 1990).

CHAPTER 7: CARING FOR COMMON PROBLEMS: DEPRESSION, ANXIETY AND STRESS

1. Joseph W. Ciarrocchi, *A Minister's Handbook of Mental Disorders* (Mahwah, NJ: Paulist Press, 1993).

2. A. T. Beck, *Depression* (New York: Harper & Row, 1967).

3. Carroll Saussy, "Pastoral Care and Counseling and Issues of Self-Esteem," in *Clinical Handbook of Pastoral Counseling,* vol. 2, ed. R. J. Wicks and R. D. Parsons (Mahwah, NJ: Paulist Press, 1993), p. 370.

4. See, for example, Melody Beattie, *Codependent No More* (Center City, MN: Hazeldon, 1987) and R. Hemfelt, F. Minirth, and P. Meier, *Love Is a Choice* (Nashville: T. Nelson, 1989).

5. Howard W. Stone, "Depression," in *Clinical Handbook of Pastoral Counseling,* vol. 2., eds. R. J. Wicks and R. D. Parsons (Mahwah, NJ: Paulist Press, 1993).

6. K. Mitchell and H. Anderson, *All Our Losses, All Our Griefs* (Philadelphia: Westminster Press, 1983).

7. Andrew D. Lester, *Hope in Pastoral Care and Counseling* (Louisville, KY: Westminster John Knox Press, 1995), p. 49.

8. See, for example, J. W. Ciarrocchi, *Why Are You Worrying?* (Mahwah, NJ: Paulist Press, 1995), or M. G. Craske, D. H. Barlow, and T. A. O'Leary, *Mastery of Your Anxiety and Worry* (Albany, NY: Graywind Publications, 1992).

9. See, for example, R. J. Wicks, *Touching the Holy* (Notre Dame, IN: Ave Maria Press, 1992), and R. J. Wicks, *Seeds of Sensitivity* (Notre Dame, IN: Ave Maria Press, 1995).

10. See Joseph W. Ciarrocchi, *The Doubting Disease* (Mahwah, NJ: Paulist Press, 1995).

11. Thomas E. Rodgerson, *Spirituality, Stress and You* (Mahwah, NJ: Paulist Press, 1994), p. 4.

12. Hans Selye, *The Stress of Life* (New York: McGraw-Hill, 1976), pp. 174–77.

13. See Sharon E. Cheston, *As You and the Abused Person Journey Together* (Mahwah, NJ: Paulist Press, 1994).

CHAPTER 8: CARING IN A CRISIS

1. Gerald Caplan, *Principles of Preventive Psychiatry* (New York: Basic Books, 1964).

2. For a more expanded discussion of the definition of crisis see D. C. Aguilera and J. M. Messick, *Crisis Intervention*, 5th ed. (Princeton: C. V. Mosby Company, 1986); David K. Switzer, "Crisis Intervention and Problem Solving," in *Clinical Handbook of Pastoral Counseling*, eds. R. J. Wicks, R. D. Parsons, and D. E. Capps (Mahwah, NJ: Paulist Press, 1985); and David K. Switzer, *The Minister as Crisis Counselor* (revised and enlarged) (Nashville: Abingdon Press, 1986).

3. For a fuller discussion see D. C. Aguilera and J. M. Messick, *Crisis Intervention*.

4. Albert Hofmann, "Psychotomimetic Agents," *Drugs Affecting the Central Nervous System*, vol. 2, ed. A. Burger (New York: Dekker, 1968).

5. For a more complete discussion see D. C. Aguilera and J. M. Messick, *Crisis Intervention*.

6. Angela Browne, *When Battered Women Kill* (New York: The Free Press, 1987), p. 8.

7. "Women and Violence," *Hearings before the U. S. Senate Judiciary Committee,* August 29 and December 11, 1990, Senate Hearing 101–939, pt. 1, p. 12.

8. Kristina Rose and Janet Goss, *Domestic Violence Statistics* (National Criminal Justice Reference Service, Bureau of Justice Statistics, 1989), p. 12.

9. P. H. Neidig and D. H. Friedman, *Spouse Abuse* (Champaign, IL: Research Press Company, 1984), pp. 61–64.

10. Lenore Walker, *The Battered Woman* (New York: Harper & Row, 1979), pp. 19–31.

11. D. C. Aguilera and J. M. Messick, *Crisis Intervention.*

12. U.S. Congress, Child Abuse Prevention and Treatment Act, Public Law 93–247. 93rd Congress, 1974.

13. D. C. Aguilera and J. M. Messick, *Crisis Intervention.*

14. See D. D. Broadhurst, M. Edmunds, and R. A. MacDicken, *Early Childhood Programs and the Prevention and Treatment of Child Abuse and Neglect* (Washington, DC: National Center on Child Abuse and Neglect, 1979), p. 2; and D. D. Broadhurst and J. S. Knoeller, *The Role of Law Enforcement in the Prevention of Child Abuse and Neglect* (Washington, DC: National Center on Child Abuse and Neglect, 1979), p. 15.

15. I. S. Lourie and L. Steffano, "On Defining Emotional Abuse" in Proceedings of the Second Annual National Conference on Child Abuse and Neglect, vol. 1, April 17–20, 1977, pp. 205–8. See also *Family Violence Packet* (Valley Forge, PA: National Ministries, ABCUSA), p. 13.

16. S. E. Cheston, *As You and the Abused Person Journey Together* (Mahwah, NJ: Paulist Press, 1994), p. 18.

17. S. E. Cheston, "Counseling Adult Survivors of Childhood Sexual Abuse," in *Clinical Handbook of Pastoral Counseling,* vol. 2, eds. R. J. Wicks and R. D. Parsons (Mahwah, NJ: Paulist Press, 1993), p. 455.

18. V. J. Fontana, *Somewhere a Child Is Crying: Maltreatment—Causes and Prevention* (New York: New American Library, 1976), pp. 58–77.

19. S. E. Cheston, *As You and the Abused Person Journey Together,* p. 27.

CHAPTER 9: CARING ENOUGH TO REFER

1. S. E. Cheston, *Making Effective Referrals: The Therapeutic Process* (Lake Worth, FL: Gardner Press, 1991), pp. 42–85.

2. M. M. Cunningham, "Consultation, Collaboration and Referral," *Clinical Handbook of Pastoral Counseling*, eds. R. J. Wicks, R. D. Parsons, and D. E. Capps (Mahwah, NJ: Paulist Press, 1985), p. 169.

CHAPTER 10: CARING FOR THE CAREGIVER

1. L. McCann and L. A. Pearlman, "Vicarious Traumatization: A Framework for Understanding the Psychological Effects of Working with Victims," *Journal of Traumatic Stress* 3 (1990), 131–49.

2. R. Janoff-Bulman, "The Aftermath of Victimization: Rebuilding Shattered Assumptions," in *Trauma and Its Wake: The Study and Treatment of Post-Traumatic Stress Disorder*, ed. C. R. Figley (New York: Brunner/Mazel, 1985), pp. 15–35, and S. Epstein, "The Self-concept, the Traumatic Neurosis and the Structure of Personality," in *Perspectives on Personality*, vol. 3, eds. D. Ozer, J. M. Healy, Jr. , and A. J. Stewart (Greenwich, Conn.: JAI Press, 1989).

3. C. Maslach, "Understanding Burnout," in *Job Stress and Burnout*, ed. W. S. Paine (Beverly Hills: Sage, 1982), p. 32.

4. J. A. Sanford, *Ministry Burnout* (Mahwah, NJ: Paulist Press, 1982), pp. 5–16.

5. See the unpublished doctoral dissertation (Loyola College in Maryland, 1994) by T. E. Rodgerson, "The Relation Between Situation, Personality, and Religious Problem-Solving in the Prediction of Burnout Among American Baptist Clergy."

6. E. B. Bratcher, *The Walk-on-Water Syndrome* (Waco, TX: Word, 1984), p. 21.

7. W. H. Willimon, *Clergy and Laity Burnout* (Nashville: Abingdon Press, 1989), p. 86.

8. A. Wheelis, *The Quest for Identity* (New York: W. W. Norton, 1958), p. 206 ff.

9. F. Stalfa, Jr. , "Vocation as Autobiography: Family of Origin Influences on the Caregiving Role in Ministry," *Journal of Pastoral Care,* vol. 48 (Winter 1994): 370–80.

10. E. A. Hanna, "The Relationship Between False-Self Compliance and the Motivation to Become a Professional Helper: Part I," *Smith College Studies in Social Work*, vol. 60 (1990): pp. 169–83; "Part II," vol. 60 (1990): pp. 263–81.

11. R. May, *Love and Will* (London: Collins, 1972), pp. 155–59.

12. R. J. Wicks, *Self-Ministry Through Self-Understanding* (Chicago: Loyola University Press, 1983), p. 42.

13. R. J. Wicks, *Touching the Holy* (Notre Dame, IN: Ave Maria Press, 1992), p. 145.

14. K. Leech, *Soul Friend* (San Francisco: HarperCollins, 1992), p. 173.

15. W. Willimon, *Clergy and Laity Burnout*, p. 96.

16. A. J. Heschel, *Who Is Man?* (Stanford, CA: Stanford University Press, 1965), p. 96.

17. K. Leech, *Soul Friend*, pp. 169–70.

18. U. T. Holmes III, *Spirituality for Ministry* (San Francisco: Harper & Row, 1982), p. 148.

19. F. W. Dillistone, *The Power of Symbols in Religion and Culture* (New York: Crossroad, 1986), p. 14.

20. Ibid., p. 6.

21. K. Leech, *Soul Friend*, p. 135.

22. See C. V. Gerkin, *The Living Human Document* (Nashville: Abingdon Press, 1984), p. 20.

23. K. Leech, *Soul Friend*, p. 171.

24. For a more complete account of friendship see R. J. Wicks, *Touching the Holy*, pp. 93–122.

CHAPTER 11: CARING FOR THE CONGREGATION

1. K. Leech, *Soul Friend* (San Francisco: HarperCollins, 1992), p. 110.

2. For a full treatment of the congregation as family system, see E. H. Friedman, *Generation to Generation* (New York: Guilford Press, 1985).

3. U. Merry and G. I. Brown, *The Neurotic Behavior of Organizations* (New York: Gardner Press, 1987), p. 5.

4. Ibid., p. 20.

5. J. Savage, *Listening and Caring Skills in Ministry* (Nashville: Abingdon Press, 1996), p. 88.

6. Ibid., p. 89.

7. See N. M. Hopkins, *The Congregation Is Also a Victim* (Washington, DC: The Alban Institute, 1993).

8. These suggestions come from R. W. Napier and M. K. Gershenfeld, *Groups, Theory and Experience*, 3rd ed. (Boston: Houghton Mifflin Company, 1985), pp. 436–39.

9. J. Savage, *Listening and Caring Skills in Ministry*, pp. 77–100.